Praise for SOL

"Tom Bryant's stories triggered my memory, and brought a smile time after time. My memories differed in detail: my cane-pole fishing was with my father on Caraway Creek in Randolph County, my water moccasin encounter was on the canals of the Broad Creek in Lenoir County and my early duck hinting was on the Currituck when there were still ducks. I could go on, but anyone who has spent time in the outdoors and stopped to look, and to appreciate, as Tom did will read these beautifully crafted stories, remember their own, and smile."

— Jack Spencer,
Retired NC Superior Court Judge
Avid bird hunter and bird dog aficionado

"Aside from being a great guy with a wonderful perspective of life, Tom Bryant is a Southern storyteller of the first order. He tells tales with great sentiment yet always avoids being sentimental."

— David Woronoff
Publisher of The Pilot Newspaper

"Enjoy the our-of doors? Wonderfully entertaining vignettes portraying the author's love and appreciation for nature's bountiful blessings. Bet you can't read just one!"

— Rich Warters, Pinehurst, NC
Retired assistant school superintendent in New York state
Avid bird hunter and deer hunter
Trains and owns the national champion English Pointer

"Tom Bryant has led a life rich with nature, wildlife, and people. He's also a talented writer who has chronicled many of his outdoors experiences in the form of very interesting and entertaining stories. These tales are a great testament to how being close to nature and people can be great fun, but also give one's life extra meaning. Pure enjoyment to read!"

– Art Rogers,
Retired former owner of one of the largest textile mills in the state
Avid bird hunter and salt-water fisherman

"Tom Bryant, the articulate sophisticated writer, AKA Bryant, is pretty famous in my circle of friends. So many memories with unforgettable quotes such as, *"Hey Bubba, hand me another one of those ham biscuits."* Then, of course, the more frequent, *"While you're back there, get me another cold one."*

The point is, how he writes and what he writes illustrates who he really is. Bryant is an optimist read for life's whatever is next. He's the nostalgic, respectful of nature, his family and friends. Though his stories, you'll get it, you'll feel it. With Bryant, you can't help but have a good time."

– Bryan Pennington,
Textile Broker, Burlington, NC
Avid bird hunter
Trainer of bird dogs including
Llewellyn Setters and Wire-haired Pointing Griffons

"Tom Bryant can tell a story- with a twinkle in his pen. Tom has walked the woods for game and for the nourishment of his soul since he was a boy. He can bring his experiences to life for those who have been with him, for those who wish they had been with him and perhaps, even for those who will never know the difference. In any event for all those who will listen to his words, the joy and wonder of the natural world will come alive.

Tom has learned lessons about the outdoors from experiences, some of which I have been a witness to:

– Concentration of the mind- from the weight of a 100 pound canoe dropped six inches and pinning your fingers on the car boat rack in 15 degrees temperature.

– Planning ahead- from the exhilaration and terror of you and some other lost soul stumbling down a 70 degree include you have never seen before in the dead of night with a canoe on your shoulders toward, and hopefully not into, the Haw River- to go duck hunting.

– Long range planning- from meticulous construction of the ultimate duck blind on the down street end of a long narrow island in the Haw completed a week before a storm surge leaves no trace to it.

These are lessons one learns on the way to mature adulthood. But why would you want to go there- how much fun would you miss."

– John H. Vernon, III, Burlington, NC
Senior Partner, Vernon Law Firm
Former President, NC Bar Association
Avid bird hunter, loves Brittany Bird Dogs

"Tom Bryant's book is the best collection of stories I've ever seen. Tom talks about hunting ducks, turkeys quail and other birds as well as deer. You'll enjoy the deer story and its conclusions. Tom also writes about dealing with young men who are doing something they shouldn't. His descriptions of all that it takes to having successful hunts is fascinating. In addition Tom also goes into a fair amount of fishing both fresh and salt and the many boat options that he and his friends put together. I recommend you read this book of outdoor living and all that goes with it."

– Frank A. Daniels, Jr. Raleigh, NC
Former Publisher, The News and Observer
Former Member, Oakland Club, SC

Southern Sunrises

Tom Bryant

Southern Sunrises

Southern Sunrises

Tom Bryant

Southern Sunrises
Tom Bryant

𝔗𝔥𝔢 ℭ𝔬𝔲𝔫𝔱𝔯𝔶 𝔅𝔬𝔬𝔨𝔰𝔥𝔬𝔭

since 1953
Southern Pines, North Carolina

Southern Sunrises

All rights reserved
Printed in the United States of America
First published as a The Country Bookshop paperback 2017

For information about permission to reproduce selections from this book
write to Permissions, The Country Bookshop,
140 NW Broad Street, Southern Pines, NC 28387

Fror information about special discounts for bulk purchases, please contact
Kimberly at The Country Bookshop 910.692.3211

Printing by Ingram Spark, Tennessee
Book Design by Judi Hewett
Production manager: Kimberly Daniels

Library of Congress Cataloging-in-Publication Data
Names: Bryant, Tom (10/07/1941)-author
Title: Southern Sunrises/Tom Bryant
Description: First Edition | Southern Pines: The Country Bookshop, {2017}
ISBN 9780999131701
Subject:
Classification:

ISBN 978-0-999-13170-1 pbk.

The Country Bookshop
140 North West Broad Street
Southern Pines, North Carolina 28387

1 2 3 4 5 6 7 8 9 0

Tom Bryant

DEDICATION

This book is for the two most important ladies in my life: Evelyn Fore Bryant, my 98 year-old mom, who taught me the love of reading; and Linda, my bride, who encouraged me to write.

Southern Sunrises

Table of Contents

Forward 1
A Boy's Firearm 3
Summer of '54 7
Old Moss 11
Summer of the Ivory Bill 17
A Weekend in the Woods 21
On the Firing Line 25
Thumbs Up 31
Swift River Seminar 35
Wild Ducks on the Haw 39
Earl's Farm 43
The Chatooga 47
Wildfowl Memories 51
A Better Idea 55
My Favorite Christmas Present 59
For the Love of a Retriever 63
Nature's Light Show 67
The Winter Storm 71
Just a Couple of Snow Dogs 75
The Cypress Swamp 81
Beloved Season, Remembered Friend 85
Maggie, We'll Miss You 89
Advice to A Young Hunter 95
A Rich Man 99

Table of Contents

The Old Man and The River................. 103
Catching Up with Christmas................. 107
Rocking Porch Resolutions 111
The Alaska Highway 115
The Perfect Stranger 121
The Great Unloading 127
The Beach Boys............................131
The "Soule" of a Good Hunt 137
Black Duck Paradise 141
Where Eagles Soar......................... 145
Dance with the Mule Deer 149
All Is Not Lost............................ 155
The Big Play.............................. 159
Three Mornings in the Spring Woods.......... 163
Dove Season 167
On Beaver Pond...........................171
Ducks Revisited........................... 175
Whistling Wings 179
Acknowledgments 183

Foreword

As modern technology continues its frenetic pace to destinations unknown, the evolving wonders of our natural world continue at a preordained but glacial pace. As humans, we find ourselves increasingly enslaved to the former though we are genetically wired in concert with the latter. Social media and internet "information" replace real human interaction and the acquisition of genuine knowledge and wisdom. The interstice is ever widening.

As you read the following pages, you will be drawn into a delightful, poignant, humorous, and inspiring world filled with real people. It is a natural world of fields and woodlands, of streams and oceans, of sun and wind, heat and cold. The stories told derive from the experiences of Tom Bryant and the collection of colorful characters he has encountered over a lifetime of hunting, fishing, hiking and discovering the endless and exciting mysteries of our exquisite world beyond computers and cell phones.

It is my good fortune to have shared many of these journeys afield with Tom. I hereby forgive him for the occasional hyperbolic rendering of detail, in itself an integral component of sporting endeavors.

Tom Bobo, former owner and CEO of Fairy Stone Fabrics, retired

Southern Sunrises

A Boy's First Firearm

It was 1951, and I was ten years old and in Mrs. Moore's fifth grade at Aberdeen Elementary. Christmas vacation was on us, and like most youngsters my age my feet barely hit the ground. What with winter camping trips with my Scout Troop 206 and planned hunting expeditions with my granddad down on the farm in South Carolina, I had little time for such niceties as eating meals with the family. "Tommy," my mother said as I ran through the house with Smut, my closest friend and companion. Smut was a curly-coated retriever my dad had given me when I was in the second grade and we were inseparable. Wherever you saw the dog, I was close by. "Supper is at six o'clock. You make sure you're home by then. We're putting up the tree tonight."

"Yes'm," I said, slamming the back door. In a heartbeat, I was on my bike peddling furiously up the street to my good friend Andy's house. Andy was sort of a neighborhood hero to the kids who lived in eastern Pinebluff because he had what every young boy lusted after, a BB gun. Of course, in those days of the fifties, lust was a word not in our vernacular. Suffice it to say, all the Santa Claus letters began with "This Christmas, all I want, Santa, is an official Red Rider lever action BB gun. I've been extra good this year." The kid in the movie, A Christmas

Story, had nothing on me except that his Christmas wish came true, and mine was delayed for about fifty years. Christmas morning came early at the Bryant house with my sisters and me charging down the stairs to see what Santa had brought. I didn't get that Red Ryder BB gun. I do remember a shiny new Schwinn bicycle along with camping gear and an assortment of other presents.

Later that morning as we were eating breakfast before our annual trek to my grandparents' for Christmas dinner, my mother asked me if I had a good Christmas. "I guess so. My new bike is great."

"Hon, I know you're disappointed about not getting a BB gun, but Santa knows that those things are dangerous. You can hurt yourself or one of your friends."

"Yes'm," I replied and thought I could still shoot Andy's.

That afternoon as we were preparing to leave the farm for home, my granddad called me back to his study.

"Before you go, Buddyrow, I wanted to talk to you for a minute. I understand that you didn't get that BB gun you wanted this Christmas."

"Yes sir, Mom thinks I could get hurt, and so does Santa, I guess."

"Well, she's right; BB guns are useless to a real hunter. All you can do with those things is shoot songbirds and you can't eat those. You know how we feel about eating what we kill."

"Yes sir, that's what my dad says all the time, too."

"You wait here a second. I'll be right back." He left the room, heading back to the side porch. I was ready to get home to my new bicycle, so I stood impatiently, balancing on one foot and then the other.

A couple of minutes later, he came back in the room with a long box under his arm. "Santa dropped this by the house last night and asked me to give it to you today. He also gave me some special instructions to go with it."

My mouth was hanging open because printed across the box was Remington Model 550-1 Semi-automatic 22 Rifle.

I couldn't believe my eyes. Santa didn't bring me a BB gun. He got me a real 22 rifle.

"Now hold on there, Bubba," my granddad said as I was pulling the rifle from its box. "This present comes with some caveats."

I didn't know what caveats meant, but I was sure it had something to do with my new rifle.

"You can't take it home with you yet," he continued. "Not until you've passed my weapon safety test and have hunted with me a few times. Your mom wouldn't like it if you hurt yourself with this rifle, and your grandma wouldn't like it if you hurt me. So here's the plan: next weekend come on back down here, we'll do a little squirrel hunting and I'll start teaching you how to handle this thing without hurting yourself or anyone else. Until then, the rifle stays here."

So that was the beginning of my lifelong association with rifles and shotguns. I've never been afraid of a weapon, but I've always respected them; and over the years (knock on wood) I've never had a close call because of that respect.

Handguns came later in life. My granddad always told me that a handgun was useless for hunting. "Even Annie Oakley couldn't hit a duck with one of those things. All they're good for is killing people."

That adage was good for the fifties but that was then; today is a little different. I was trained with and fired my first pistol in the Marine Corps, and after that obligation did not fire another one until years later.

A couple of weeks ago, I pulled an old Smith and Wesson 38 police special out of my gun safe and decided to take the license-to-carry course and see what it was all about. Several of my friends had taken the course up in Alamance County and were hauling pistols around in their trucks in case they ran up on a bear or something. I couldn't let them get one up on me, so early one Friday morning I arrived at Ed's Gun Shop ready to take the course under the capable tutelage of Dwight Creech.

Dwight is a medium-sized fellow with a professorial look, and his license-to-carry class was taught better than many of the classes I had in college. His actual profession is education, and he's the principal at Calvary Christian School. He grew up on a farm in Johnson County and attended East Carolina where he majored in psychology and got a master's degree in philosophy. A lot of his education and Christian beliefs bleed over into his course, and after a short conversation, I could tell that he's a dedicated man. I immediately respected him for that. The course was from nine o'clock until about five, and then we went to the pistol range at the Moore County Wildlife Club to fire approximately fifty rounds at different distances from the target. Sixteen people participated in the class, and I believe everyone passed both sessions.

Passing the course is just the first part of the process. Next would be getting an application from the sheriff's department for a concealed handgun permit and completing all the many North Carolina requirements. When this is finished, submitted and approved by the state, the permit would be issued in about six weeks.

I've yet to start the second part of this process and really don't know if I will. A handgun is great for family protection; but for hunting, like my granddad said about Annie Oakley, I still couldn't hit a duck with one.

Summer of '54

"Tommy. Tommy. Tommy, TOMMY!"

"What?"

"I have to go to the bathroom." We were perched in my dad's 1951 Chevrolet Deluxe like a bunch of nervous yearling birddogs getting ready to hunt. My sister, Bonnie, age six, was the one with the immediate problem. She was leaning over the front seat with a real anxious look. Billie, my other sister, age eight, was on the other side looking out the driver's rolled-down window toward the realtor/rental office where my father and mother were. My brother, Guery, age four, was up in the ledge of the back window saying over and over again, "I want to go to the beach. I want to go to the beach. I WANT TO GO TO THE BEACH!" I, Tommy, age thirteen, was in the front seat trying to maintain some semblance of order with my younger siblings, while Daddy and Mother were inside dealing with the rental guy. It was August 1954, and we were at Ocean Drive Beach for our annual summer vacation. I was rapidly getting a major case of claustrophobia after riding for four hours in a car crammed full of antsy kids and enough summer beach gear to last a family of six for two weeks. I was pretty antsy myself.

The beautiful blue, rolling Atlantic Ocean, in all her majesty, was just a couple of blocks away. I could even hear the big waves as they slowly crashed on white sand beckoning us, "Hurry, hurry, you're missing it."

"Bonnie," I said to my uncomfortable sister. "Mother will be out in a minute and she'll take you inside to the bathroom. So calm down." My brother was still on the back window ledge trying to drive me crazy, saying his beach mantra over and over again. Mother finally came out of the office and took care of Bonnie while Dad got some last minute rental information from the agent in charge. Then we were off to check out cottages.

That's the way it was done in the early fifties at South Carolina beaches. No need for reservations. When you got ready to go to the beach, you went. After you got there was the time to find a beach cottage. In those days, the little beach towns were sleepy crossroads waking up when summer came and boarding up when the cold winds blew down from the north.

It's ironic when I think about it now; the tide that changed the way things operated was the winter wind whistling in more than cold weather. It also blew in frigid souls from places like Ohio and Pennsylvania and Canada. Once those folks found the beautiful, unspoiled stretches of white-sand beaches and slow rolling blue waves, the little towns with the names Cherry Grove, Ocean Drive, Crescent Beach, Windy Hill and Myrtle Beach would never be the same. Dad and Mother always got the keys to three or four cottages, and we would drive down the beach to see if they fit the family's criteria. As far as Mother was concerned, the house had to pass muster with two major requirements: a big screened porch and plenty of windows facing the ocean. Oh, the house also had to be oceanfront, none of this sound-side location stuff for her. Dad was only concerned with the cost and whether there was enough room to handle a relative or two who might visit during the week. And the cost? I can remember that a hundred dollars a week was at the top end of what my dad would pay. He tried to talk the rental guy down to seventy-five; or if he was real lucky and things had been slow for the agent, he might even get the cottage for fifty. Fifty dollars in those days was a lot of money. The time spent inspecting the cottages to pick just the right one was torture for four kids who were required to the stay in the car. Our parents were smart enough to know that releasing all of us before the beach house was chosen could extend the effort a lot longer than their cursory inspection would take. Once out of the car, getting all of us back in would be like herding cats. Part of my duty was keeping order and controlling my brother who was trying to make a break for it out an open backdoor window. It didn't usually take long for Mom to choose the cottage she wanted. After that, we would unload, and Dad would take the extra keys back to the rental agency. Then we would settle down to a wonderful two weeks' stay. Unfortunately, Dad could only spend the night before having to return home for work. As superintendent for City Products, an ice plant designed to ice railroad produce and peach cars for trains moving north, July and August were his busiest months; and rarely could he be spared from the plant for more than a day or two at a time. He would try to get back to the beach as often as he could.

Beach cottages at that time were simple affairs without air-conditioning. They had hardwood floors, big porches, covered decks, wide windows and ceiling fans, so laid back comfort was as near as the closest rocking chair. On this summer vacation, I had the best of all worlds. The bedroom I shared with my little brother had a huge double window opening right onto the screened porch. I arranged a folding cot outside the window, and during the night I would crawl through the opening, wrap up in a summer quilt and let the ebb and flow of the ocean waves rock me to sleep.

My first year as a teenager was all I hoped it would be, and this summer vacation trip to the beach was icing on the cake. After the first couple of days, the family settled into a routine. I would wake early and just lie on my cot soaking up all the wonderful sensations: sounds of sea gulls crying, accompanied by the crash of the slow rolling tidal change; pelicans, on the way to favorite feeding grounds soaring over the house using the updraft of warm, ocean breezes; and probably the best morning awaking call of all was the rich smell of frying bacon and eggs as Mother, busy in the kitchen, prepared for another day.

As it happened that summer, the family was able to stay at the beach for an entire month. A favorite aunt of mother's visited and liked the place so much that she rented the cottage for the additional two weeks. The only caveat was that we stay with her during those final days of August.

The summer of '54 was one that I'll always remember. Like most of that decade, it seemed to be a peaceful, gentle time. Looking back, it was as if the country was taking a break, resting after World War II and the Korean War and maybe, without knowing it, gearing up for the tumultuous time ahead. On the trip home after that wonderful time at the beach, my sisters and brother slept soundly in the back seat of the car. I sat on the front bench seat between Mother and Dad. School was to start in a few days and I had a lot on my mind.

"Did you have a good vacation? Dad asked as we motored down the highway between fields of tobacco.

" Yes, sir, I replied."

"Do anything different?"

"No, sir." He chuckled and said, "I'm glad you had fun." My ninety-five year old mother often says there is a season for all things. That summer season, my first as a budding teenager, was one of the best.

Old Moss

"*Now don't you go wandering off from this spot, son. I'll be back around 10:00 to pick you up.*" We were on the Holwell Plantation for my first real deer hunt. Not really my first deer hunt but the first time my grandfather actually let me man a stand by myself. I had been with him before but just as a watcher. Today I was one of the hunters and felt almost grown. I was thirteen.

The Holwell Plantation backs up to Black Creek Swamp, which joins the Big Pee Dee River Swamp. This is one of the wildest areas in the state and actually begins what's known as the low country of South Carolina. My grandfather's deer club dated back to the early 1900s. Membership was small including a lot of relatives who I only got to see around deer season every year. Members of the club provided the land for the club to use. There were big family farms with enough land to hunt an area one week and then shift to another farm the following week. It was an honor to be invited to hunt with the club, especially for me, a youngster with a shotgun as long as I was tall. I wasn't a novice, though. Numerous outings with my father and grandfather had taught me to handle a rifle and a shotgun.

"Teach 'em early and they won't forget," my grandfather would tell my mother when she would raise an objection to my having a gun at a young age. "Why, I was providing meat for the table when I was eight years old."

In the south, wild game harvested went a long way toward supplementing table fare. After the War Between the States, during reconstruction, an impoverished population's harvest from the rivers and fields often meant the difference in going hungry or not. It was a lesson remembered, and my granddad's deer club was a hold-over tradition from those days. There was a respect for wildlife bordering on the religious. In many cases, crops were planted specifically for game. Two or three rows of corn would be left standing, and food plots for quail and other birds would be planted in wild areas to make sure the animals had food for the winter.

It was a great time to be a kid with all those grownups treating me as an equal. The morning of the hunt, I watched as the members were assigned stands from numbers drawn from a hat. I expected to join my granddad again and just watch and was too surprised to say anything when my Uncle Tom came over to where I was sitting on the back of a pickup gate and offered me the hat to draw a number.

"Granddaddy already has a number," I said questioningly. My uncle looked at me and smiled. I noticed the rest of the members looking my way.

"Yep, that was his stand. You've got to draw for yours." My mouth fell open, and I looked from my uncle to my granddad, who was standing close to the truck.

"Go ahead, son. It's time you showed these old-timers how to deer hunt." Thus began a day I'll never forget.

A southern deer hunt during that time used dogs, and my granddad had some of the finest in the area. His string included Blue Ticks, a couple of beagles crossed with some other hounds, he even had a bloodhound mix in the group, but the most unusual was an Airedale that my aunt from Texas had given him for Christmas. That dog was one of the best. My grandfather didn't believe in pets. If an animal lived on his farm, it had to produce. There was no free ride.

A typical hunt started with the hound master putting out the dogs in a likely area where deer had been spotted the day before. This was after everyone had time to get to their stand. And once on the stand where you were to hunt, you did not move from that area. That was extremely important. Nothing could get you kicked off the field faster than leaving the stand before the hound master signaled the hunt over. There was one member voted out of the club for going to the dogs, no pun intended, after being warned several times. He also had one of the largest plantations, down close to Georgetown, but it made no difference. It was rumored that on a later outing on his own property, he was accidentally shot while trying to follow the dogs. The hound master is the only hunter who can roam, and this important position is rotated within the club. Usually the most experienced hunters assumed that responsibility and shared the duties every week. Blowing a cow horn that had been hollowed out into a bugle signaled the end of the hunt. It's amazing how far that baleful trumpet could be heard.

I was a proud youngster when my grandfather dropped me off at my stand with a few last instructions. The morning was cold with a heavy frost, but I was too excited to feel it. My spot was in a little cut the shape of a half circle right next to a fenced pasture. There was an old fallen oak tree that would make a natural hide, I thought, and I loaded my shotgun, really my father's, a JC Higgins pump. Earlier, I had cleaned the gun so much that my father accused me of rubbing off the bluing. I hunkered down close to the base of the ancient fallen oak and prepared to watch and wait. To this day, I attribute my patience in the woods to those early times at my grandfather's hunt club. Every second was an hour. I could hear my heart beat. I think my ears actually grew as I tried to discern what every noise, every rustle in the bushes could be. A squirrel chattered, a crow called, and then silence. After a while that seemed an eternity, I heard the dogs. They were way back in the swamp and I was on the ridge, not a good spot. My grandfather always told me that a dog-jumped deer would head to water and safety, and I could hear the baying moving more deeply into the swamp.

A big Black Angus bull came to the fence of the pasture and looked over at me as if to ask what was I doing in his neighborhood. I tried to scare him away but only attracted more cows. I think they thought they were going to be fed. What a predicament. Here I was, a big time deer hunter, being watched by a herd of cows. In the distance, I could hear the dogs turn. It seemed as if they were heading toward high ground. They got louder, and then the baying receded toward the swamp again.

I've got to get rid of these cows, I thought. They'll scare all deer away. I propped my shotgun on the oak stump and walked through the little clearing to the fence and shooed the cows out into the pasture. I was halfway back to my gun when the deer came blasting out of the woods running flat out. Big? I've never seen anything so big before or since. He had his head back with a rack of horns resting on his shoulders the size of my grandmother's rocking chair. He cleared the fence of the pasture with room to spare and was across it and gone before I could shut my mouth. I stood there a minute dumbfounded. How had that happened? My shotgun rested uselessly next to the oak, and I was standing in the middle of the clearing when the dogs came howling through. I felt like throwing up. Later after the hound master sounded the end of the hunt, my grandfather came by for me. We were in his pickup on the way back to the clubhouse, and he asked me if I had seen the deer.

"Yes sir, I saw him and could have got him if I'd had my gun with me." I explained what happened.

"I'm proud of you, son," he said smiling. "You could have shot some cows if you'd had your gun when "Ole Moss" came tearing by. Now don't you worry about it. Your Uncle Fred saw him too, and he had his gun, shot three times and missed. We're gonna cut off your uncle's shirttail. A cut shirttail is a tradition that goes way back and is reserved especially for deer hunters who have a good shot, fire, and miss. The back of the shirt is cut off with scissors and tacked up in the clubhouse. One wall of the ancient log barn that served as headquarters for the hunt club was covered with shirttails of every description.

Later, after we picked up the dogs and were on the way home for dinner, my granddad said, "Tom, that big old deer you saw today is kind of the club's mascot. He's been around forever. Even if a member gets a shot at him, it's an unwritten rule that we miss. We only shoot to scare him and keep him on his toes. That's what your uncle Fred sacrificed his shirttail for today."

I hunted one or two more seasons with my granddad before sports and other things grabbed my attention. The hunt club long ago disbanded as the farms were broken up and sold. Most of the old-timers I hunted with have passed on to their great reward, but I like to think that somewhere in the deep, dark, cypress swamp of the Pee Dee River, one of Old Moss's great-grandsons still roams.

Old Moss

Summer of the Ivory Bill

Every now and then, just as the lemmings head for the sea, I've got to find me a black water river to wet a South Carolina jig. This urge comes naturally, since my maternal grandfather, Austin Fore, instilled it in me.

Our favorite haunt was his old fishing camp located on the Little Pee Dee River pretty close to Gallivants Ferry. If you've ever traveled to Myrtle Beach on Highway 501, you've crossed the river at the ferry. When your car rumbled over the bridge, you were only 10 or 12 miles, as the crow flies, from the old fishing camp where I spent some of my happiest time as a youth. The summers were mine in those days. I had yet to get a job. "Let him have some fun, Evelyn," my granddad would say to my mother. "He's got the rest of his life to be responsible and work. Let him come fishing this summer with me. I'll teach him a few things. And besides, I need a paddler." That was my last Tom Sawyer summer, filled with idyllic days fishing, paddling and observing nature in its almost pristine form. There was one early evening when we were slowly drifting back toward camp. As Granddaddy had promised, he had taught me to paddle, and I was in the stern of the boat, keeping her in line with the bank so he could toss his jig under the low hanging alders. We had a boatload of fish, and I had put my rod down and was enjoying the slow drift, moving the paddle back and forth propelling the boat from side to side without making any noise. He taught me well.

"There's nothing, Son, that'll run off a fish more than a fool with a paddle. You don't have to splash and turn the river into a froth to move a boat. It's all in letting the water do the work."

A bird flew over the river and landed in a huge cypress. He was slowly pecking on the side of a dead branch. Unlike a regular woodpecker, his efforts knocked bark down as if he were swinging an ax. My granddad whispered back to me as he slowly boated his rod, "Just be real quiet and watch."

The woodpecker was big, probably a little bigger than a crow. I marveled at how much the bird looked like the movie cartoon character, Woody Woodpecker. He hung to the side of the dead branch almost upside down, his white beak slowly pounding on the tree. When we were right under him, he dropped off the branch and soared away, beating his wings in a way that kind of loped him across the swamp.

"Son," Granddad said, "You've seen what few men will ever see again, an ivory-billed woodpecker. They used to frequent this swamp, in fair numbers. This is the first one I've seen in years. Maybe it's a good sign and they're coming back. Who knows? Anyway, you saw him and I bet you won't forget him."

That fall, my granddad had his second heart attack, a bad one. "One more like this," the doctors said, "and we'll not be able to help. He's got to watch his diet and stay away from strenuous activity." After that great summer, I only saw my granddad at holidays and when he would visit occasionally. A few years earlier, our family had moved to Pinebluff. My dad was working all the time supporting a family of four kids, and he spent most of his waking hours at the ice plant in Aberdeen. He was the superintendent, and during peach season all of his time was dedicated to his job. Fortunately for me, Pinebluff was made for kids. My parents couldn't have picked a better town for us to grow up. There was only one problem. I loved to fish, and the only fishing water I had access to was Pinebluff Lake where we swam and hung out all summer. The lake was great for that kind of entertainment, but for fishing, I could have caught as many casting on Highway One. I put my fishing equipment aside and concentrated on baseball.

One early summer evening, Dad and I were sitting on our front porch. I was in the swing, and he was kicked back in a rocker. My sisters and brother had gone to bed, and Mother was in the kitchen doing the supper dishes. Later on, Dad was going to work to check on the night shift, and I was just enjoying this time with him. It was quiet with just a little breeze whispering through the pines, and lightning bugs flashed here and there.

"What are you up to tomorrow, Sport?" he asked as he lit a cigarette.

"We don't have a ball game, so I think I'll get up early and try fishing down at the lake, for whatever good that'll do me. I've fished every corner of that pond and haven't caught a thing but a couple of turtles." Why don't you and your buddies look into Drowning Creek?" My dad suggested. "Now, don't go down there. Just talk to some of the adults in Pinebluff about the fishing. I know Mr. Mills would know all about it. He knows everything about this area. Your grandfather always said that the Lumber River is a great place to fish. Remember, he and your Uncle Hubert fished up around Whiteville that time and caught a cooler full of redbreast. Drowning Creek is actually the headwaters of the Lumber, so there's bound to be good fishing."

The next morning that's exactly what I did. Johnny Mills was a good friend, a year or two younger than I, but we still hung out together. His dad was the mayor and the go-to guy for information about almost anything concerning Pinebluff.

"I don't want you boys to go down to that creek without an adult," Mr. Mills said, "It's a good fishing spot but loaded with big ol' cottonmouths. Later on this week, I'll drive you all down there and we'll check it out."

And that's how Johnny and I became acquainted with Drowning Creek. In a couple years when we grew a little bigger, the creek became one of our favorite destinations. Sterling Carrington and a few other boys from the southern part of the county actually made a swimming hole at Blues Bridge. No swimming for me. I could just picture all those hungry cottonmouths. But the fast flowing water became my special fishing hole.

The summer before my senior year in college, my grandfather had his third heart attack while fishing the Little Pee Dee. The doctors were right. This one took him away. After the funeral, Mother and I drove down to his fishing camp. The rest of the family stayed at the farm to help greet visitors. When we arrived, Mother went inside and I wandered down to the dock where my granddad kept his boat.

The boat still had his tackle box and two or three bait casting rods in it. I got in to retrieve his fishing gear so I could store it in the cabin. This boat was a brand new one that I hadn't seen before, so I climbed back in the stern, sat down, and grabbed a paddle. The river flowed quickly creating a small eddy, moving the boat slowly side to side on its ropes. I turned the seat so I could lean back and see upstream. There was a great big sand bar that thrust out in the water at the bend of the river, and a giant cypress grew right at the edge. The sun was at its highest point, and all the animals and birds were hunting shade. There was a flicker of white in the very top branches of the cypress, and I wondered what bird was moving at this time of day. After a minute or so, the bird soared across the river and turned toward the bend. There was a lot of white showing on its wings, and it had the unmistakable flight of a big woodpecker. It slowly flew around the bend and out of sight. And I remembered that great summer when my granddad taught me to paddle and we were deep enough in the swamp to see the ivory-bill.

A Weekend in the Woods

"Sometimes you find yourself in the middle of nowhere, and sometimes in the middle of nowhere you find yourself." Anon

I guess you could say that it was a growing year for me — character, experience, age — all three coming together my first year away from home. Prior to entering Brevard College, I had been what you might call a medium-sized fish in a small pond.

Aberdeen High School, student population 300, was the perfect place for me, a reasonably intelligent student who leaned a little too much toward sports to the detriment of studies. I did enough to get by, though, with the help of coaches and dedicated teachers.

The administrators at Brevard were quite clear. "Tom," the dean of students said, "tests show you have the intelligence to do the work. The desire is up to you. We've talked to your coaches and principal at Aberdeen and they agree with us, you have the potential to be a good student and perhaps have an opportunity to play baseball for Brevard. It's up to you. We're going to give you a year to make the grade. This is not high school. It's the first step in your future and only you can make this year work."

The seriousness of the situation lay across my shoulders like a wet blanket as Mother and I drove home after our weekend visit to the school. Mother was unusually quiet as we headed down the mountain. She spoke up as we neared the small town of Bat Cave. "Well, Tom, what do you think? He meant what he said. You either make it this year or you don't."

"I plan to give it a try," I replied. "You and Dad have sacrificed to send me to school. If I don't make it, then I wasn't supposed to be there in the first place." That fall I hit the ground running, putting in the hours on the books, studying like I'd never done before. And the good grades came. I was burning up everything except biology, and although I was doing okay in my class work, I still was not actually becoming an active part of the student body. I didn't make friends as readily as I usually did and still felt too much like an outsider. Studying all the time, worrying about making the grade in biology, and just in general missing the entire crowd at Aberdeen High, I was pretty miserable. Homesick was the word.

Then one day in biology lab, I was dissecting a frog and something was wrong. I'd had plenty of experience cleaning game: ducks, squirrels, and rabbits. Never before had I had a problem with blood or animal innards, but this pickled frog seemed to get to me. Time to have a serious chat with the teacher, I thought. Dr. Lobdell, my biology professor, was a unique individual, a wiry little gray-headed lady of indeterminate age who ruled the class with an iron hand. She put up with no foolishness and I had tried to remain below her radar, until now. After lab I stopped by her office in the administration building, and as I approached the door, I could hear her on the phone, so I waited right outside in the hall. "I didn't call you to listen to your problems. Someone is cutting wood on my property without permission and I want it stopped. I don't care if you have to send a deputy out there to spend the night. It has to stop!" She hung up the phone with a bang. Whoa, bad timing. I decided to beat a retreat; but before I could ease away, I heard, "Come in, don't just stand out there. Come in."

"Tommy," she said as I stepped in the doorway, "I'm glad you came by. It's time we had a little conference about your lab work." The conversation went a lot better than I had anticipated. Dr. Lobdell became more a caring person and less the ogre I had thought her to be.

"I'm assigning my assistant to help you in your lab work which might mean you're going to have to put in extra time, but it should make a difference in your grades."

Our talk ventured away from studies to a little more of a personal nature, and I expressed my desire to get in the woods, maybe do a little wandering in the mountains, hiking or camping. I jokingly said that all this studying was making me a dull boy. That brought up the problem of her land and the interloping woodcutters.

"I don't know what I'm going to do. The sheriff doesn't have the manpower to send a deputy, and whoever is doing the cutting has already ruined some good specimens."

"I've got an idea," I replied. "What if I go out there this weekend, do a little exploring and see if I can figure out who the culprit is. It would be fun for me and might solve your problem."

The next weekend found me, at last, back in the woods. Dr. Lobdell's property covered about a hundred acres and backed up to the Pisgah National Forest adding another few thousand, plenty of room to roam. The weather, for that time of year, was unusually mild and I packed light, just a sleeping bag, tarp, and a bag full of goodies that Dr. Lobdell had prepared for me.

I didn't have a fire that evening so as not to alert the trespassers, and I made a few reconnoiters from one end of the property to the other to no avail. No one showed and I crawled into my bag soon after midnight.

A little before dawn, I was awakened by a chain saw that sounded as if it was on the far north end of the property. I silently sneaked over the ridge and saw what appeared to be a couple of teenagers chopping on a freshly cut locust tree. They were intent on their work, and the noise they were making enabled me to ease around the back of their rusty hulk of a truck. It was a good thing I did because an ancient thirty-thirty rifle was propped right beside the open door. I picked up the rifle, leaned on the front fender, and waited for the boys to notice me. I scared the bejesus out of the pair.

"What! Who are you?" the boy nearest me asked as he looked up from his wood-cutting. He still had an ax in his hand so I planned to play it by ear and see how this scenario was going to work.

"Put the ax down and you guys come over here in front of the truck." I stepped back just a little and the pair did as I said. I put on my best country drawl. "You boys are in a heap of trouble. The sheriff is gonna show up in about thirty minutes and tote y'all off to jail." The two ragged boys whined disclaimers like a backwoods lawyer.

"We didn't do anything wrong. We've been cutting wood here for years. I pointed over to a No Trespassing poster on a near tree. "Can y'all read that?"Somebody must have just put that sign up. It wasn't here yesterday."After a while of scaring the boys sufficiently, I unloaded the rifle, handed it to the nearest youngster and said, "I'm gonna give you a break and let you go, but if I even hear of a limb cut anywhere on this property, I'm gonna come get you."

The two loaded up and beat a hasty retreat down the fire lane that served as their road.

That semester I passed biology, which enabled me to make the dean's list. I'm sure Dr. Lobdell's assistant and her added instruction were the reason, but the weekend I spent camping on her mountain had to help a little.

On the Firing Line

Tendrils of smoke drifted across the charred forest ground every now and then, turning into tiny yellow flames. At dark we stopped venturing out with our five-gallon water spraying cans to put out the flare-ups. It seemed useless, since the firebreak was supposed to hold back these little flares and the heavy underbrush fuel had already burned, leaving nothing but a choking, smoldering mess.

"Where did Poochie go?" I asked.

David, sitting on a rotten log on the edge of the freshly dug firebreak, answered, "He said he was gonna go down to the base camp to see if he could get a couple more sandwiches. You know Poochie, always hungry."

What had started out as a lark had turned into several days of drudgery. "You know I kinda wish that we had never signed up for this duty. If I had known it was gonna be this much hard work, I would've stayed back on campus."

David and I were roommates our sophomore year at Brevard College. The school is located right on the edge of the Pisgah National Forest, a beautiful wild mountain land where we hiked and camped on many occasions. I looked over at Dave. There was a full moon and the burned-over forest was visible in an eerie, desolated way.

"Yep," he repeated as he scratched at the fresh dirt left by the bulldozer with a limb that was burned on one end. "I don't know whose idea this was but it was a bad one."

I laughed and tried to get more comfortable. I was sitting on the ground leaning against a cut made by the dozer.

"Think back, Dave. It was your idea, remember?"

He didn't, but I sure did. It was right after mid-term exams during the dead of winter. It was snowing to beat the band and Poochie and I were in his room commiserating about the history exam we had just finished and hoping we had passed, when David came sauntering in. He had a four by five card in his hand that looked official. "Here it is, guys. Our way to fame and fortune this spring."

"I'm ready for the fortune," Poochie replied. "I've got enough fame. Whatcha got there?"

"It's a query card from the forest service. They're looking for a few good men."

We both laughed at the irony. We had just been talking about joining the Marines after graduation.

"No listen. Here's the drill. In the spring when the forest fire threat is the greatest up on Pisgah, the forest service signs up a few students to keep on stand-by in case they're needed. And here's the great part, when they put you on alert, you get paid even if you don't go. And those folks pay good. You remember Anderson? He graduated last year. I was talking to him about it and he told me he had participated and made over a hundred dollars and didn't even leave the campus. All he had to do was just be here in case they needed him. I mean where can you make money just sitting around?"

"Yeah," Poochie replied, "but what do you do if they need you?"

"They pick you up, haul you where you need to go and feed you. That's what Anderson said."

"How did he know? You said he never left the campus."

"They told him, that's how. Before you can go, there's a briefing you have to complete." We found out later there was a lot more to it than just signing up. First an applicant had to be in good health, and second and more important, grades had to be such that a person could miss several days of classes if needed. Poochie, Dave and I, along with a couple of other fellows, fit the bill, were accepted and really didn't think that much about it until spring approached and the fire season was upon us.

"Well, they took us and here we are right in the middle of it." Poochie said as he walked out of the gloom with a bag full of sandwiches. I don't know where he got his nickname and never questioned it. He was just Poochie. It fit.

"Jack said he would try to get us out of here and back to school tomorrow."

Jack was the ranger in charge of our area of fire control and was right on top of everything. I don't think he closed his eyes the whole three days we were on the line.

"Anyhow," Poochie said, "I'll take the first watch. Tom, you can relieve me, and David can have sunrise duty."

All we did while on fire watch was just make sure that nothing unusual happened in our area of control. The fire had just about burned itself out and we had no real qualms. Our biggest problem was staying awake.

The next morning dawned grey and smoky. A watery looking sun tried to break through the haze. We met as a group at the couple of tents that had been home base for the last few days. Jack drove up in an old army Jeep. He had been checking in with the other rangers down the fire line.

"We've got one more job to take care of before I can take you boys back to campus. I'll only need one, and the rest of you can start breaking down the tents. Tom, why don't you come with me? Bring your water can and make sure it's full. Guys, we'll be back in a short while."

After filling my water can, I climbed in the back of the Jeep, and Jack backed up and headed down the mountain. He looked back at me and hollered over the noise of the vehicle as it whined down the rough dozer cut. "We've got to start a back-fire on the other side of this mountain. It should be simple enough." In no time, Jack pulled the Jeep off the firebreak across from what appeared to be a dry creek bed.

"Okay, Tom, here's the plan. We're going to move down this bed a ways and then double back. I'll have the fire starter and you follow along with the water sprayer to make sure things are burning right. The brush is thick here and the fire should catch and hold. It'll move up the mountain and burn up the fuel that the fire that's rolling on the other side of the ridge would need. Ready?"

We walked about a hundred yards down the natural break. There were a few areas where we cut down brush that hung over the dried up creek. "This ought to do it. I'll start the burn right here." Jack lit the kerosene fire burner and started along our path. I was right behind hauling the water can. We were about half way back to the Jeep when a weird noise got our attention. Jack stopped and stood looking up the creek bed. The noise was getting louder and sounded like the whine of a low-flying jet. I was watching Jack for a clue as to what was going on when his eyes got big and he set down the burner, grabbed my arm and shouted, "Drop the can and RUN!"

My feet were already moving when I shouted back, "Well, get out of the way!"

A freak gust of wind had blown the backfire to the opposite ridge creating a chimney effect down the dry creek bed rushing the fire directly towards us. Needless to say, Coach Cohen, our baseball coach, would have been impressed with my speed covering the last fifty yards to the firebreak and safety.

Later that evening back at school and after a good hot shower and a great dinner, the three of us were in Poochie's room talking over the experiences of our four days at the mountain fire.

"What do you think?" David asked. "There's a lot of fire season left, should we re-up with the forest service?"

"Not me, Dave," I replied. "I can still see and smell that runaway fire roaring down the creek bed toward us. I wasn't really scared until I saw Jack's eyes. And later when he said we'd had a close call, it was too close for me. I'm just glad we had the Jeep and could get out of there. I don't think I'll even get near a fireplace anymore. Take my name off the list."

Thumbs Up

No responsible sporting organization has ever sanctioned this outdoor sport. Most folks wouldn't even consider doing it; but if you happened to be player when you were young, wild and foolish, then you know what I'm talking about.

It began in the late forties, reached its heyday in the fifties, and peaked in the early sixties. With the advent of interstate highways and two cars in every driveway, the sport withered on the vine and became a fond memory to those of us who were participants.

The sport of hitchhiking, gone forever with the occasional exception of a few down and outers, was a way many of us moved from one location to another when we were still in school.

I started thinking about the fine art of bumming a ride the other evening while I was watching the old movie, "It Happened One Night," with Claudette Colbert and Clark Gable. In one scene, the couple was stranded along a country road and Gable was showing Colbert the fine points of catching a ride. He used every gambit from the confidant I-don't-really-care-if-you-pick-me-up-or-not thumbing motion to the desperate-emergency-I-need-a-ride gesture. Nothing worked until Colbert used the old raising-her hemline-to-straighten-a-stocking-seam and vehicles locked up their brakes.

Colbert's technique never worked for me; although in some wilder locations where I've been stranded, it might have.

During the fifties, it was not unusual to pick up a hitchhiker on the way to Aberdeen and pick up the same person on the way back to Pinebluff. It was a way of life and part of the benefits of growing up in Moore County. Most of the time, drivers who picked us up were friends of the family and, more often than not, would drop us off in front of our houses. So it was not rare to see young people on the side of the road with their thumbs gesturing in the wind. Hitchhiking was a male sport, though, and females were discouraged from participating. I can't ever recall seeing a girl hitching a ride until the mid-sixties when equal rights became an issue. This occurred toward the end of the sport, though, and was probably a good thing. After high school and before Dad bought me my first car, I moved up a step in the sport and began hitching rides back and forth to college. I attended Brevard, a small junior college in the mountains, and it was not unusual for me to step out on the side of Highway 1 in Pinebluff at ten o'clock in the morning and be in my dorm room by three o'clock that afternoon, about as fast as my dad could drive me. Of course there were little ways that a college student could help his situation. Most of the time we were catching rides with strangers, and even in those trusting days, they needed a little reassurance that you were on the up and up. I always wore a tie and a blazer. I had a small suitcase that had a Brevard decal on the side, and I would make a cardboard sign indicating that I was a student on the way back to school. It always worked.

When I was a sophomore, my dad bought me a 1940 Chevrolet Deluxe, a great old car that served me faithfully for many years. But back then, even though gas was 35 cents a gallon, I couldn't always afford to fill her up. So I would continue to use my expertise in the thumbing sport to save nickels.

I learned early that when hitching across country it's important to have a back-up plan. So I always stashed away enough money to catch a bus if I was stranded or in a bad situation. A couple of times that emergency fund came in handy. I met some great people during my travels. I found that ninety percent of them were basically alike. They all aspired for the same things and had good hearts. The other ten percent? I always hoped I wouldn't get in their cars. But sometimes I did.

After graduating from Brevard and entering Elon College, my family moved to Lakeland, Florida, which was a long way to hitch a ride. By then, however, I considered myself somewhat of an expert and decided to thumb home during semester break. It was to be a real adventure, going and coming. My roommate dropped me off on the other side of Graham, NC, wished me well and headed to his home in Raleigh. I immediately caught a ride to Sanford. The driver was a deacon in the Baptist church and was on his way home after visiting a relative for the weekend. He wanted to make the eleven o'clock service and let me out on the new bypass around town. I stood around for awhile. Not much traffic on Sunday morning. One of the beauties of hitchhiking in those days was being able to notice the small things along the side of the road. On one trip I even found a twenty-dollar bill just lying in the grass. I whiled away the time in between rides making up stories about that cash. Cars were few and far between. I was meandering southward at a leisurely pace when I heard a car, out of sight, screaming my way. Good grief, I thought, that fellow has his foot in the carburetor. When he came over the hill and saw me, he slammed on brakes and skidded past me to the side of the road. The car was a brand new Plymouth Fury hardtop convertible. A guy opened the passenger door and hollered back at me; "Hurry! Hurry! Get in the back! Let's go!" I ran to the car, tossed my suitcase in the backseat, and climbed in as the driver roared off, both tires smoking as he burned rubber. Uh-Oh, I thought. I might have made a mistake here. I was looking for the seat belt as the passenger leaned back and introduced himself and his partner. "Hope you don't mind but we're trying to break our time record from Chapel Hill to Ocean Drive. Hang on. Would you like a cigarette? No? How about a martini?"

They were students at UNC and did indeed break their record. I was glad when they let me out on Highway 17 south of Ocean Drive Beach, and I was glad that I had finished the ride in one piece.

A friend had lent me the use of his beach house whenever I was in the area and I took him up on it and spent the night at OD, as we called the little beach north of Myrtle. I sacked out early, planning on a fresh start the next morning to continue my epic trip to Florida. This particular hitchhiking adventure was toward the end of my thumbing career, and I met other interesting people along the way. For example, there was a fellow who picked me up right outside of Charleston. He was driving a little Nash Metropolitan, one of the smallest cars on the road. He was nipping a little from a pint whiskey bottle that he kept under the seat, so I talked him into letting me drive. He nipped along all the way through Georgia and fell asleep just south of Jacksonville. He had advised me shortly after I got behind the wheel that the brakes didn't work too well and to use the hand break as much as possible. That got my attention as we coasted over the Savannah River Bridge and came to a screeching halt at the stoplight right before town. I almost yanked the little hand brake out of its socket.

The journey back to school after spring break was just as hair raising. It had a promising start when two co-eds in a bright blue convertible picked me up. I rode with them to Gainesville, Florida, then caught a ride to Jacksonville with a good old boy in a pick-up with no muffler. It took an hour before my hearing came back.

Then the ride to beat all rides was the one with a pair of newly married Seminole Indians heading to Waycross, Georgia. They were still celebrating when I climbed in the car. After a few miles, I encouraged them to let me drive while they partied. But that's a whole other story.

I finally made it back to Elon and resolved to give up the sport of hitchhiking and do something a little more sedate. So I joined the US Marine Corps. The whole time I was with them, I didn't have to worry about a ride.

Swift River Seminar

It is difficult to find in life any event which so effectually condenses intense nervous sensation into the shortest possible space of time as does the work of shooting, or running an immense rapid. There is no toil, no heart breaking labour about it, but as much coolness, dexterity, and skill as man can throw into the work of hand, eye, and head; knowledge of when to strike and how to do it; knowledge of water and rock, and of the hundred combinations which rock and water can assume.... Anonymous

Our 17-foot Grumman aluminum canoe was lodged on a pair of immense boulders, bent like a pretzel; and river water was washing gear, a piece at a time, downstream. The immediate task at hand was to save ourselves and then as much of the equipment as we could. The "we" in this crowd included Phillip Motley and me, lifelong outdoor people and excellent river paddlers, or so we thought, and our good buddy, Dick Coleman, eminently qualified to handle the chore at hand, which was to survive. Phillip and I were in the Grumman canoe, and Dick was in an inflatable kayak. We were on the Haw River, normally a free flowing easy paddle; but like Doctor Jekyll and Mr. Hyde, she could change her stripes with the water level rise of just a few inches.

Our river outing was to paddle from Swepsonville, North Carolina east to where the Haw River and the Deep River join to form the Cape Fear, and then on to Wilmington and the mighty Atlantic. We figured about eight days of camping and easy paddling. Wrong on several counts. We hadn't considered two weeks of heavy rain just prior to our launching date. Worse than that, we hadn't done our homework on how the Haw River could change with just a little rain. Vacations arranged, gear packed, plans made, we looked at the rising river and opted to go. The first of many mistakes.

After being swamped and overturned numerous times, we were exhausted and a long way from a take-out point. Our gear was soaked, and loading and unloading the canoe after all the dumping had sapped our strength. We didn't realize it until much later in our whitewater experience, but the rapids that we made it through on that first day were high 3s and mid 4s on the whitewater scale of difficulty and danger. The scale only goes as high as 6, and to run a rapid of that number only gives a 30% chance of surviving. We were not in a place for novices. Philip and I were able to get a rope from the battered, impossibly lodged canoe to a small island in the middle of the river. We hand-walked the rope back and forth from the boat to the island, hauling supplies as we went, and were able to save most of them from washing down stream, at least for a while. Our small haven in the middle of this maelstrom was about four feet wide by maybe thirty feet long, and the river was rapidly rising. Our buddy, Coleman, was nowhere to be seen. We'd lost contact shortly after our canoe was swamped and lodged against the rocks and now faced a sleepless night on the island with only one thing for sure; and that was, in the morning, we were going to have to swim for it.

Morning dawned grey, cold and wet. Rain had started again shortly before daylight. Our little piece of dry land was almost under water, so we roped what was left of our gear to a small tree, tied the canoe to the same tree, put on our life jackets and swam for the west bank. And that, folks, is how we were introduced to whitewater paddling. Sort of on-the-job training or learn-as-you-go, something I don't recommend to anyone. But after our experience on the Haw, or better said, our survival, we recognized what a great sport paddling an open canoe in whitewater can be and were determined to learn how to do it right. We lived through our first experience without too much trouble. The catchword here is lived. Phillip and I were able to hike into town where we found our compatriot safe and sound. Unfortunately, we had messed up the morning for several rescue squad people. I couldn't tell if they were more disappointed that their mission was called off or happy that we were alive. I think the former. In those days, there wasn't a lot of excitement in Pittsboro.

We did manage to turn back the helicopters they had ordered from Fort Bragg before they arrived. Also, Dick had refused their suggestion that he call our wives and tell them that we were dead. Smart boy, that Coleman.

Later, after the river receded, we were able to salvage the canoe; but our gear was long gone. Coleman always lamented the loss of two bottles of first class Jack Daniels Tennessee Whiskey that were in our duffel. We always laughed about it later that somewhere on the Haw were some very happy fish.

Eventually, four or five of us got into whitewater canoeing in a big way, and just about every weekend would find us paddling somewhere. We also discovered that the Haw was a great learning river with rapids that required quite a bit of technical skill, and we honed our expertise before graduating to rivers that required more experience. The canoes stayed in the garage, though, when the Haw was running high.

Philip and I paddled tandem for a couple of years until the urge to strike out solo pushed us into buying canoes especially designed for whitewater. He got a Mad River boat, and I bought a 16-foot Kewadin, a round rocker-bottom canoe that would throw you like a skittish stallion if you were not on your toes. All that practice and the new boats put us on some major rivers such as the Nantahala, the New, the Chattooga, the Toe, the Gauley, and the Haw, even when the water was almost at flood stage. The skill we developed enabled us to paddle waters that we would never before have attempted.

White water canoeing is a great sport, but it's still dangerous; and at the insistence of my bride to take up a hobby that doesn't require so much life insurance, I hung my Kewadin canoe in the garden shed. It's out there right now gathering dust. But you know, that little canoe is as capable as she always was; and every now and then when I cross a bridge over a whitewater river and see the rapids, I wonder if I am.

Wild Ducks on the Haw

The Haw River begins as a couple of small springs in Forsythe County and flows through Guilford, Alamance and Chatham Counties to the Jordan Dam. On the downriver side of the dam, the Haw joins the Deep River to form the mighty Cape Fear that flows to Wilmington and the Atlantic Ocean. At one time or another, I've paddled most sections of that long stretch of water. On one trip when the river was at flood stage, I swam through a lot of it chasing a canoe. But that's another story. This is a tale about duck hunting on a small part of the Haw from Swepsonville to Saxpahaw in Alamance County, NC.

In the early fifties on through the mid-seventies, the Haw would often run blue with foam as high as two feet in some areas of the river. The foam came from textile mills along the banks that used the flow of the water as a dumping ground for their wastes. When the Clean Water Act regulated wastewater disposal, the river cleaned itself up a little. Actually, not just a little, a whole lot. The Haw hasn't reverted to its pristine quality of the early days and probably never will. The population of the river basin is too dense. But in the seventies and eighties when I spent a lot of time on its waters, the clean-up was most welcomed.

My good friend John Vernon and I cut our duck hunting teeth early on an eight-mile rocky section of river between Swepsonville and Saxapahaw. John was a big quail hunter, having hunted his grandfather's farm in Person County as a youngster just as I was a small game hunter, also having hunted on my grandfather's farm in South Carolina. So we had the love of the outdoors in common.

John and his lovely bride, Vicki, had moved back to North Carolina after he had completed graduate work at New York University. He then began working with his father at their Burlington law firm. I had just started a small weekly newspaper and, needless to say, John and I were up to our eyeballs in our respective careers. We weren't so busy, though, that we couldn't spend a few Saturdays quail hunting. On one late fall hunting trip up to John's home place, he brought up the idea that we should try our hand at duck hunting.

"Tom, I've got a client who has a farm on the Haw River. Last week we were talking about bird hunting and he said that he didn't have quail on his farm anymore, but when he was down close to the river the other morning, he jumped about a couple hundred mallards. They were evidently feeding on acorns that floated down the little creek that runs through his farm. He said we could come down there and hunt anytime." Thus it began, our obsession with one of nature's finest creations, the wild duck.

The following Wednesday afternoon, I picked up John at his office and we drove down to the old gentleman's farm to get the lay of the land. We needed to find a place to launch the canoe for retrieving ducks if our hunt was successful. The sun was close to setting so we didn't have a lot of time to reconnoiter before we ran out of daylight. I parked where the dirt road dead-ended, and we walked down through the woods. The terrain slanted downward at a pretty extreme angle the closer we got to the river. "I don't know, Tom. This could be rough, hauling a canoe in the predawn dark with all the gear. We'd even have to cross this fence before we get to the water." We climbed over a broken-down hog wire fence and came to the river that was flowing at a lazy pace.

"You're right. We'll have to make a couple trips, one for the canoe and one for the gear. So we need to get here early, especially since we don't know where we're going on the river. Hey, look! There they are!" We happened to be standing back in the tree line and the five mallards landing in the river couldn't see us. Across about twenty yards of water was a small spit of an island covered in thick brush and stunted trees. We could see the downstream point of the island, and the ducks that had just landed swam around it and on down the river.

"Can you believe it, Tom?" John whispered. "We have just stumbled onto our future duck hole. This is where we need to be Saturday morning. By the way, are we gonna eat breakfast before we hunt or after?"

Breakfast always plays a big part in a successful day afield, and the ones we enjoyed in those days were something to behold: bacon or country ham or both, eggs cooked any way, redeye gravy, grits with loads of butter, biscuits soft like grandma used to make, and strong, stand-up-a-spoon black coffee. I believe that the reason breakfast is still my favorite meal comes from those early duck hunting days. Now, though, it has been whittled down to healthier cereal and blueberries.

Four-thirty the next Saturday morning did find us conducting what we later called a Saxapahaw Chinese fire drill. The canoe bounced off trees and scraped across brush as we dragged it to the river. In the blackness of pre-dawn, we struggled to keep our balance and sense of direction.

"Well, where is the cotton-picking river?" I asked after spending what seemed an inordinate amount of time trudging and hauling.

"We're going the right way unless the river started running uphill," John replied. "Here's the fence, so it shouldn't be too much farther. There it is."

The river ran cold and dark not twenty yards from where we stood. "Man, I don't want to do this every morning. We've got to find another place to put in," I said. "A fellow could break a leg on this trek."

"Let's check the river later before we take out," John replied. "There's got to be a better way."

And there was. After an unsuccessful morning hunt where we saw a lot of ducks heading downriver and flying too high for shooting, we picked up the measly half dozen decoys that we had haphazardly thrown off the point of the little island, and paddled upriver to search for a better launching point.

"That must be the creek that flows through the farm," John said as we rounded a bend. A small cut in the bank with clear water gushing into the muddy river looked like the place that John's friendly farmer had told him about.

We paddled up the little creek about fifty yards and pulled the canoe into a slough. An overgrown path ran up the hill to a pasture with Black Angus cows grazing near a small house.

John said, "If we can drive across that pasture, we've got it made."

"Yep, let's head back, load up, and go talk to your friend and see if he'll let us cross his pastures. Maybe you can cut him some slack on your hourly fee."

As it turned out, the old gentleman did give us access to his farm, and we successfully hunted the Haw for several more years until circumstances took us to more diverse hunting locals such as our own duck impoundments overlooking the Pamlico Sound. Our hunting style has changed over the years. We're a little longer in the tooth, and our hair has thinned and grayed around the edges, but we still have the same enthusiasm that continues to roust us out of a warm bed at four o'clock on a frosty January morning. It helps just as it did on the Haw in those early years to know that a duck hunter's breakfast goes with the hunt.

Now when we make hunting plans the evening before, we always go over particulars such as where to put the decoys and how many we'll use, which blind to hunt, what the weather will be like, how warmly to dress, and how many shells to take. Important stuff like that. But I can still hear John asking about the most essential part of a successful duck hunt.

"Are we gonna eat breakfast before or after?"

Earl's Farm

We were in a real pickle. I had one leg over the barbwire fence balancing the canoe with one hand and the other hand was trying to keep the barbs from some very important body parts. My hunting partner, Dick Coleman was on the safe side of the fence holding the other end of the boat, urging me on. "Come on, Bryant, it's getting dark. We need to get on outa here." The here was a little creek in the northern part of the county that helped fill the county's water reservoir, and we were just coming off of it after a very successful duck hunt. We were in unfamiliar territory and had never hunted this part of the county. As a matter of fact, Dick had found the spot just the day before the season opened and hoped it could really pan into a good place to hunt during the year.

Our scouting for likely duck holes was really very simple. We would ride around out in the country about sundown, find a swampy low area, park the truck, and watch to see if ducks were using it for a roost.

Dick had actually stumbled across this little stream with its banks covered in hardwoods by accident. Taking a short cut on the way home from work one evening, he heard some unusual noises coming from his old Blazer and pulled off the side of the road to investigate. It was just a loose fan belt, something he could take care of when he got home. As he closed the hood, he looked up and saw about a dozen mallards, wings locked, feet down, dropping into a shallow slough that ran under the little bridge that was just ahead.

He called me later that evening. "Bryant, you're not gonna believe it. The ducks were swimming back and forth under that bridge like they were on parade. I sneaked over the fence that's right there on the side of the road and watched them until it was almost too dark to see."

"It sounds great, Coleman," I said, "but that's the city lake and it's out of bounds. You can't hunt there."

"Nah, you got it wrong. That creek just feeds the lake. We're nowhere near the big reservoir."

"Yeah, but somebody owns that property. You had to cross a fence, you said. We don't have permission to hunt."

"Come on, Bryant. Free flowing water belongs to everybody. All we have to do is get to it. Look, the season comes in tomorrow. We can go back to our usual place and just watch a beautiful sunset without even loading the gun, or we can hunt here and shoot some ducks! I say hunt here. I'll pick you up tomorrow afternoon around four. It shouldn't take more than an hour to set up and get ready for the evening flight."

"No, let me pick you up," I replied.

"I've already got the canoe on top of the Bronco. All I've got to do is throw in some decoys. And maybe after we hunt, we can find out who the land belongs to and get permission."

"Yeah, yeah, right. Shoot up some guy's farm and then see if we can find him to tell him that we were the ones doing the shooting."

"I'll leave that up to you," he replied. "You're always good at that kind of stuff."

Coleman was born too late. If he had come along during the era of mountain men, he would have put Jim Bridger to shame. Always out of doors, hunting, fishing, camping or canoeing; if he wasn't doing it, he was planning on doing it. We had a lot in common, but perhaps I was a little more tempered on the conservative side when it came to risk-taking. I had just got the canoe and then myself over the barbwire fence when up the hill we could see headlights coming our way. A pick-up truck came around the curve, slowed when his headlights framed us like prisoners making a break, drove across the little country bridge to where I had parked my Bronco, turned around and slowly drove back toward us.

"We're in for it now," I said to Coleman.

"The fellow in that truck looks as if he means business."

The pickup came to a stop just this side of the little bridge and a man stepped out holding a flashlight. He left the truck idling and his door open. "How you fellows doing?" he asked as he surveyed us with his flash. See you been hunting. Have any luck?" I put my end of the canoe down. Coleman still held on to his, mesmerized. He looked like a deer caught in headlights. I figured I had better step up and say something.

"Yessir, we were getting in some ducking right here before the sun went down. We got a limit. It sure is a pretty place down here."

He shined the flash on me. I could make out he was a heavyset gentleman with a work jacket, jeans and brogans. He had a cap on and I couldn't see his eyes.

"Where you folks from?" Coleman still stood mute holding his end of the canoe. I answered and finally Dick came to life and we played who do you know. We were fortunate because we had mutual acquaintances, and the conversation went from an inquisition to a more friendly talk.

"I own the farm on this side of the creek all the way up to the top of the hill," the farmer said. "I've got Black Angus cattle in the pasture across from my house and tobacco planted on the back side."

"It sure is a nice looking farm," Coleman said, "and we're sorry if we trespassed. We were just trying to get to the creek."

"Yeah. Well, do y'all deer hunt?"

"No sir," I replied, knowing that Coleman deer hunted, but I didn't want to push our luck. We hunt mostly ducks, turkeys, doves and quail, when we can find quail."

"Well, you're out of luck with quail. I haven't seen a partridge around here in years. And I'm saving the deer for me."

The truck was still grumbling in idle as if it wanted to get back on the road.

"OK. Here's the deal. Get all your stuff loaded and stop back by my house. It's up there on the left."

He turned his flashlight off and walked back to the truck. I just knew he was going to have a deputy sheriff waiting with a summons when we got there. He got in, shut his door and lowered the passenger side window. I could see his face illuminated just a little by the dash lights. He was grinning at us.

"I want to give you a key to my pasture gates so the next time you come you won't break down my fences."

For the next fifteen years, I hunted what became known simply as Earl's farm. Earl eventually sold out to developers, bought a big Grady White boat and moved to the coast. Friends tell me the farm is now a beautiful housing development and that I should check it out. I don't want to. I would rather remember it the way it was, one of the finest and most beautiful places I've ever hunted.

The Chatooga

I reached out as far as I could to do a paddle brace; the stroke was familiar but my new canoe wasn't. It seemed cumbersome compared to my old whitewater boat, but hey, what did I expect? This is a lake canoe, an Old Town Discovery designed for stability. It's exactly what I need to fish the bay waters of the Chokoloskee, but it's gonna take a while to get used to it, I thought. I pulled the paddle back in and watched as a pair of dolphins surfaced and blew right off the bow.

It's a good boat, but not quite the same as the old days. I leaned against a boat cushion in the stern, made myself comfortable and thought back to those times when I was a little younger, paddling a faster boat, on the last and best whitewater river of my career, the Chattooga. It was almost like a dream; I could see and hear it just like it was yesterday.

A roaring noise, not unlike an angry surf blowing during a storm, rolled up-river, echoing from one side of the canyon wall to the other. It was an ominous sound, an all too familiar one I've heard many times, but it still creates a nervous, tingling sensation down my spine. It is the soundboard of an immense white-water rapid announcing its presence just around the next bend. Whitewater canoe and kayak paddlers are a superstitious group, a lot like baseball players. Some will use the same paddle, enter the river with the same routine, or maybe carry their first homemade bailing bucket. On this river, one of the top whitewater rivers in the southeast, I needed all the help I could muster; so my homemade bailing bucket, cut from a thick plastic gallon milk jug I found on the Haw River, was tied securely to the middle thwart.

Superstitions aside, before paddling a whitewater river, I've found that my body tightens up. It's a lot like before the whistle sounding the opening kickoff of a football game or the first pitch received while batting in a baseball contest. Once the pitch is thrown, the ball kicked or the first stroke of the paddle, the old body gets squared away and is ready for whatever comes. The real difference in this analogy is that, most of the time, a sport like baseball or football will not kill you. A raging whitewater river with class 4 and 5 rapids will.

We were paddling the Chatooga, the last on a string of East Coast Whitewater Rivers on our list. We had worked our way up the ladder saving the best or worst, as it were, for last. We had paddled the Haw, Pigeon, Nantahala, Elk, Mayo, New, Nolichucky, and Toe rivers, and the Chatooga was the last one for me.

We were a varied group, a couple of bankers, a haberdasher, a furniture salesman, a stockbroker, and myself, a newspaper ad man and outdoor sports writer. We were in our thirties, experienced in the outdoors, most ex-military and responsible family men. We also had one other thing in common, we loved whitewater paddling. I promised Linda, my bride, that the Chatooga would be my last adventure on a major river, and I planned to keep that promise. There had been some close calls on the earlier paddled rivers, and I knew that skill would only carry me so far. There's a lot of luck involved and I had already used up a bunch. Therefore, after this one, I planned on hanging up my rapids paddle and just enjoying the laid back easy-going rivers and lakes. The Chatooga is one of the longest and wildest free flowing rivers in the southeast. James Dickey's book Deliverance, later made into a movie, put the river on the map, some think for all the wrong reasons. Several unfortunate paddlers, not up to speed to tackle any whitewater river, much less the Chatooga, ended up paying the ultimate price. It is not a river for amateurs.

We made it through all the rapids without too much trouble. I took on a lot of water in the "Roller Coaster" but was able to eddy up behind a big boulder and bail. The "Keyhole" is next, I thought, and then the kicker, "Bull Sluice."

According to Bob Benner in his book Carolina Whitewater, "The entrance rapid to Bull Sluice is a class 3 which can splash a great deal of water into the canoe before ever arriving at first falls. The hydraulic below first falls can easily hold a body or a boat in so give it due respect. Keep in mind several drownings have occurred here."

My reverie was interrupted to watch a string of pelicans lazily fly over the mangroves out to sea, and I grabbed my paddle and said, "Time to break in the new boat." My verbalization to no one reminded me of an old habit of talking to myself while running heavy rapids, and as I slowly paddled in my new, comfortable Old Town Canoe soaking up the sun and surveying all the beauty in that southern Florida bay, I talked myself through Bull Sluice again. "OK, eddy to the right bank." I did a cross-draw paddle stroke, turned the canoe and hugged the bank tightly. I had made it down the entrance rapid without taking on a lot of water and took this time to look down river to first falls of the "Sluice". Breathing deeply, I eyed the entrance to the falls.

"Too much to the left and you're in the rocks, too much to the right and you're in the hydraulic. OK, peel off slowly and line the boat to the center of the chute."

The noise of the rapid was such that I couldn't hear myself as I did another cross-draw and entered the main current. My angle looked good, but the problem was the entrance to the first falls changes with the level of the river. All afternoon the river had been rising due to thunderstorms in the headwaters. What had been a class 4 was rapidly edging to a class 5. My approach looked good as I did a deep-pry stroke to push me more to the left. "Get ready!" I hit the chute too far to the right and as the boat began to roll, I did a paddle brace, to no avail. I was tossed out of the canoe, into the hydraulic, rolling around like I was in a washing machine. There was nothing to do except pull myself in tightly and hope the Sluice would throw me out like a ball. It seemed like minutes, but really I was in the Sluice for only seconds before I was flushed out like so much unwanted garbage. My swamped canoe, no worse for the wear, was resting on the right bank, being held there by another paddler; and as I swam up to him the stranger said, "Man, you were lucky! A student from Georgia Tech drowned in that hydraulic two weeks ago." As I clung to the side of my canoe, I could only smile and reply, "I know."

Those years are long gone. Lifestyles change and so do priorities; and as I dug in with my paddle and headed back to the campground, I thought about Linda back at the little Airstream getting ready for early cocktails at the tiki hut on the bay. After that I planned to grill freshly caught sea trout for supper.

The Chattooga is still rolling along in all its whitewater beauty. I've seen it and I've paddled it and I'll never forget it. That's enough for me.

Wildfowl Memories

"Nobody ever got any younger, because if they had I would have heard of it, and maybe bought some. So what a man has got to do is take a little time off as he grows older, and devote the waste space to remembering the things he did that he maybe won't never do again. And when you get tired of thinking about all the things you've done, you can always use the time thinking about what you'd like to do in the future." Robert Ruark - The Old Man And The Boy

It was March, not my favorite month. Hunting season was over and it was too cold to fish. The only redeeming feature of the month was our annual trek down to the fish camp on Chokoloskee Bay below Everglades City in Florida. The sky was slate gray, supporting a northeast wind spitting a cold rain that would probably turn into sleet before nightfall. Most everybody who had any sense was hunkered down by a fire. It was as if winter was gonna give us one more blast, so we wouldn't forget who's boss. I had been working on the little Airstream camper, trying to get her ready for our Florida adventure, but when the cold numbed my fingers, I decided to retire to the den, build a fire and kick back for the rest of the afternoon. I picked up one of my favorite outdoor books, The Old Man And The Boy, by Robert Ruark, settled into my leather chair and just happened to turn to the chapter on memories. Not a bad idea, I thought and decided to try a little experiment with one of my own memories, Canada goose hunting on the Eastern Shore of Maryland. January was the time, shortly after Christmas. My good friend and hunting companion Tom Bobo had organized the hunt for six of us at Bill Meyers' farm, Plimhimmon, located on the Tred Avon River close to Oxford, Maryland. Meyers' place was a classic Maryland plantation situated on about four hundred acres. It was a working farm, raising crops for the market in the summer. In the winter, it became a Canada goose hunting location without equal, registering such notables as Bing Crosby, Ted Williams and Phil Harris. I considered myself to be in high cotton, hunting on the same farm as such celebrities.

Five of us, John Vernon, Jim Lasley, Tom Bobo, Dick Coleman and I left the home place early on a frosty January morning for the ride up the coast, over the Chesapeake Bay Bridge and then across the Eastern Shore of Virginia to Easton, Maryland. We were crammed into Coleman's Blazer with enough shotguns and gear to outfit a squad of Marines. I remembered a photo made during the hunt and headed to the sunroom to see if I could find it in one of our albums. I got sidetracked hauling in some more wood for the fire. I was burning seasoned oak, and it was toasty warm in the den. The photo was in the first album I pulled from the bookcase, and it is a classic. The picture shows the six of us; a friend of Bobo's had also joined us. We were lined up after the hunt with our guides and the black Lab, Rebel. Bill Meyers snapped the shot. Outside the wind was really whistling, and sure enough, a little sleet mixed with snow was pelting the den windows. I put another log on the fire, made myself comfortable, looked at the photo made so many years ago and remembered that time on Plimhimmon when the six of us limited out on geese.

We stayed at the venerable old Tidewater Inn in downtown Easton. The hotel was built with hunters in mind. The restaurant and bar had wooden carved ducks and geese along with paintings depicting waterfowl hunting scenes. A huge walk-in fireplace anchored one end of the cavernous lobby. Walnut paneled walls were also adorned with classic duck and goose hunting paintings. There was always a fire in the fireplace, usually with a sleeping retriever as close to the warmth as he could get.

We ran into snow just as we crossed over from Virginia to Maryland, perfect goose hunting weather; and as soon as we registered at the hotel, Tom got in touch with Bill Meyers who instructed us to show up at the farm the next morning at seven. He also said geese were everywhere, so we should have a good hunt.

And he was right. The guides placed us in two side-by-side hedgerow blinds, three men in each one. We barely had time to load the shotguns when our guide Renny said, "Get ready, here they come."

A group of twenty to twenty-five geese was coming directly at us over the cut cornfield. They were about thirty feet off the ground and were locked in on the decoys.

Renny whispered, "I'll tell you when to take 'em, and don't everybody shoot the same goose."

We didn't. Canada geese rained from the sky. One even fell in the blind almost cold cocking Coleman. The limits on Canadas in those days were three a day, and we limited out with that one flight. Back at the barn, Meyers, who had been watching us with binoculars, said he had never seen anything like it. Plimhimmon is gone now. Meyers died, and the son-in-law broke up the farm for condos and vacation homes.

I haven't been back, but a friend who visited the area recently said the Tidewater Inn doesn't allow dogs anymore. It's just not the same. A strong gust of wind blew more sleet against the den windows, and I put another log on the fire. I've had my day with Canadas on the Eastern Shore, I thought. Now to think about things I want to do in the future just like Ruark said in his book. Tomorrow, if the weather breaks, I'll begin loading up the little Airstream.

A Better Idea

"*Bryant?*"

"Yeah?"

"I've got a great idea."

"Coleman, every time you get a great idea, I either get in a lot o' trouble or it costs me a lot o' money."

We were kicked back on the porch at the Wildlife Club after a great morning jump-shooting ducks on the Haw River. It was a classic kind of hunt. Everything came together at just the right time. The water on the river was at a good level with the current flowing fast enough to keep us on our toes but still a leisurely speed enabling us to enjoy our surroundings. And what surroundings they were. Hickory trees were decked out in all their yellow glory backed up by golden-leafed oaks. Bright green colored cedars added a perfect backdrop providing a classic early morning fall picture, something that you only see if you're lucky, or sometimes in sporting magazines. It's a classic way to duck hunt, jump-shooting from a canoe. We put the boat in at the mill dam in Saxapahaw, and using an electric kicker, motored up stream to the confluence of the river and a little creek at Swepsonville. We then floated slowly downstream, hunting as we drifted along.

Wood ducks like to swim close to the shore dabbling for fallen acorns or berries that grow near the bank. They silently float under overhanging alders and, when disturbed, will burst from their feeding space like a covey of quail. The sport, in hunting out of a tipsy canoe, is not to flip over when the duck zips out from under the alders. It's almost like shooting from a skateboard. One wrong turn and a hunter can hit the drink. Poor form, especially when the temperature is hovering around forty degrees and the truck is a couple of miles away.

Usually when I'm jump-shooting, I'm all by my lonesome. I'll only get in a canoe with another hunter if his experience in paddling a boat and his competence with a shotgun is as good or better than mine. You don't get second chances with a shotgun or a fast flowing river.

With Coleman, I had the best of both worlds, a superb canoeist and a magnificent gun handler. I've marveled more than once at some impossible shots he made in the field. I definitely wouldn't tell him that, though. We've been friendly competitors since our early days when we became close friends.

With two hunters jump-shooting from a canoe, there are a couple of very important rules — number one and the most critical, only one shooter at a time. Number two, silence is more than golden, it can be the difference between a successful duck hunt and just a float down the river.

On this trip, Coleman was to be the first shooter. We cut a few branches from a cedar tree and rigged them to overhang the bow of the boat. My canoe was camouflaged anyway, but the cedar would provide a little more cover. We wanted to look like a tree floating downstream. On the first flush, Dick got his limit of two wood ducks, a hen and a drake. He made a great double, getting both ducks as they were crossing left to right. They actually jumped from the left bank and crossed right in front of the canoe. That's the fun in jump-shooting; a gunner never knows where they'll come from.

We rapidly picked up the floating ducks and made it to the bank to change over, Dick now in the stern and I in the bow. I got my limit with a couple of singles, two wood duck drakes, the last one right at the take-out where we had left the Bronco. It was too early in the season to try again for mallards; and since we had our limit of wood ducks, we picked up and decided to head to the Wildlife Club and a pot of good coffee.

Dick Coleman was an amazing individual. I met him early in my settled-down life. I was just out of the service, back in college and married to a beautiful, smart young brunette. I had a part time job at the local newspaper, and Coleman was busy managing one of his family's men's specialty stores. We were friends right off the bat, especially when we found out about our service in the Marines. Dick was at Parris Island about three months after I left the basic training camp, and he coincidently was in the 1st Battalion and had the same drill instructors. We could really commiserate with one another, and we became fast friends.

Dick got up from his chair to get another cup of coffee. "You want to hear my great idea or what?"

"I hope it's not like the last great idea that almost got us killed on the same river we got those ducks this morning."

"Nope, this one's more sedate, and that river trip last spring was as much your doing as mine." The river trip we were talking about was one that we made after careful planning: float the Haw to the Cape Fear River, then to Wilmington and the Atlantic Ocean. A great plan, but with one problem: when we put the canoes in at Saxapahaw, the Haw River was at flood stage, and quickly chewed us up and spit us out. On that adventure we learned a valuable lesson about white-water paddling and surviving an angry river.

"Christmas is just a few weeks away. What if we get Vernon and Lasley and the girls, and have a fantastic Christmas game dinner. We've got plenty of game. I know you've got lots of doves and ducks in your freezer; so have I. Vernon's got a few pheasants. I think Lasley has some venison somebody gave him, and we could get together the fixin's with no problem. It would be simple."

"And where do you plan on having this little cookout? That close to Christmas, I know the ladies would pitch a fit if we suggested having it at one of our houses."

"No, man. Right here. We'll have the feast right here at the Wildlife Club."

"Dick, this place is just a little better than a warehouse. I mean, look at it. It's all right for a bunch of guys, but to bring Lida and Linda and Vicky and Libby? Man, they would have us scrubbing this place before they'd set foot in it."

"You're the writer. Where's your imagination? We'll make it a black-tie affair. You know, not a whole lot o' light, we'll use candles, white tablecloths, a blazing fire in the fireplace. We'll decorate, we'll have a Christmas tree, we can cut one of those cedars up by the skeet range, and holly, there's plenty of that next to the pond, full of berries. We'll send fancy invitations to the girls and make it a real dress-up shindig."

Believe it or not, it all came together the Saturday before Christmas. The ladies came dressed to the nines in long gowns that would be more suitable at the country club than out in the woods at a sportsmen's simple clubhouse, and the guys cleaned up a lot, sporting tuxedos. It was quite an affair, and turned into the first annual game dinner that I would continue for the next 35 years. It was one of Coleman's better ideas.

My Favorite Christmas Present

I grew up around boats. Not the big ocean-going ones like Grady White produces, but more like backwater skiffs that are at home on tidal creeks and inland lakes. I learned to swim in Pinebluff Lake when I was about seven or eight years old; and shortly afterward, my granddad taught me to paddle his small creek boat on the Little Pee Dee River. From then on, I was at home on the water.

Granddaddy had a bunch of boats, but one I really remember was a dug-out cypress canoe about eighteen feet long with a forty-inch beam. Where it came from, no one really knows. It was just always there. My uncles said that a low country Indian tribe made it long ago and Granddad found it sunk in a little lake off the river. He raised the craft and towed it back to his fishing cabin where he pulled it up on the bank, let it dry out for several months, then put it back in the water. It sat right on the surface like a water bug, dry as dust. Then he rigged it so it would carry a ten-horse Johnson kicker and was off to the races. I can remember the old dugout carrying four adults, three coonhounds, and me with plenty of freeboard. After my grandfather passed away, an uncle inherited the dugout, and I believe he has it stored in an old barn on his farm.

Later, as I grew older and hit the creeks again, I bought a seventeen-foot aluminum Grumman canoe. I paddled rivers, lakes and duck holes with the reliable boat and still have her perched on a couple of sawhorses behind the garage. One of my chores, on a list that gets longer every day, is to sand blast the old peeling camouflage paint that's still flaking off her sides and put her back on a black-water river this spring.

My next craft was a white-water, sixteen-foot Kewadin canoe that carried me down some mighty rough rivers. From the Haw at flood stage to the Chattooga of Deliverance fame and a bunch more heavy-water rivers in between, we skipped right over the waves. Old age ends a lot of endeavors such as white-water paddling, and the little boat is hanging from the rafters in the garden shed as good as she ever was; but unfortunately, her handler has been put out to pasture. I'll probably sell her this spring, hopefully to a youngster who will keep her as good as I tried to do. Christmas of 1983 was one of my best. Santa Claus brought me a little twelve-foot Wigeon duck boat all rigged to go hunting. It was a great surprise. My bride arranged for the skiff to be delivered to the home of my good hunting buddy, Bubba. On Christmas day and after all the folderol at our house, Linda reminded me that we were to drop by Bubba's for an afternoon holiday get-together. Several of our friends were supposed to attend. Bubba lived in a beautiful home completely fenced with a seven-foot brick wall. He had hidden the duck boat in his garden building where it would be out of sight. The afternoon hurried by, and after a great time talking to friends about the holidays and planning future duck hunts with my duck hunting comrades, we had to take our leave to get home for another function that evening.

Bubba walked out to the Bronco with us and, as I fired up the old truck, he said, "Wait a minute there, Cooter. Santa Claus left a present here for you last night. He said that his reindeer were tired of hauling it all across the country and I was to get it to you this afternoon. Come on back here and I'll show you."

We walked around to his garden house. Linda had a big smile on her face and said, "I wonder what it could be?"

I opened the door to the little building and there it sat, a Wigeon duck boat in all its glory. Linda and Santa have surprised me more than once, but this was a beauty. The little skiff and I were destined to have a grand time on lakes and rivers across the state, making memories. One from the next Christmas stands out more than most.

I was hunting at Hyco Lake, a cooling lake for a Duke Power plant, a few days before Christmas with my yellow lab, Paddle. The weather had been clear but unusually cold, so we were afraid of ice in the headwaters but knew that the lake would be open around the power plant. The Wigeon has a very low profile and wide beam. Her semi-v hull and shallow draft makes her very stable; and with the seven and a half horse mercury kicker, she's easy to get up on plane. At full speed, the boat scoots along at about twenty-five miles per hour. On this winter morning, though with the possibility of ice, we cruised along at a little under planing speed.

The lake, as we thought, was open around the plant, and we pulled into a narrow canal that fed water into the cooling towers of the huge building. A cove spread to the north off the canal, and I set out a block of mallard and black duck decoys in a small slough. I pulled the little boat close to the bank, anchored her and covered everything, including Paddle and myself with an old grey tarp. Paddle had her head stuck out of the tarp on the port side, and I leaned back against the kicker as low as I could. We sat and waited. Every now and then Paddle would whine in anticipation but would quiet down when I said, "Shhhh."

The moonless night had been as clear as a bell and a million stars were visible. The Milky Way lived up to its name stretching across the sky like a bucket of spilled diamonds. I sat and watched. Morning is my very favorite time of day. There's a promise there, a newness, and I'll never get over the breathtaking beauty as nature comes to life after a winter night's sleep.

The horizon became a little more pronounced as night turned gray in the east, ready for the sun. The silence was calm and comforting as

Paddle and I waited quietly in the little boat.

From our earliest hunting forays, I realized Paddle could spot a duck long before I could, so as the day began to brighten, I kept my eyes on her. She was something to watch. She was so tuned in to her surroundings, she almost hummed like a high-tension wire. I wasn't surprised when, as usual, she spotted the first flight. They were high. Hundreds of them, stretched out in Vs to the north as far as I could see.

Divers! They could be canvasbacks, I thought, but probably ringnecks. I could tell by the fast wingbeat and the way they didn't hesitate as they flew on to unknown destinations. We watched as flight after flight hurried south.

"Surely some of these ducks will take a rest on the lake," I whispered to Paddle. She looked back at me as if to say, "Yeah, when?"

As suddenly as they appeared, the ducks were gone.

We watched until the sun was high in the sky, and then as if by mutual consent, Paddle and I decided it was time to go. I folded the old tarp, picked up the decoys, cranked the kicker and headed the Wigeon back toward the landing. As I brought the little boat up on plane, Paddle looked back at me and seemed to be grinning. I said to her over the noise of the motor and spray, "How about all those ducks, Paddle?"

Her answering bark said it all.

For the Love of a Retriever

Dick Coleman was the fellow who started it all. The dog business, that is, or more exactly, the retriever dog business. For a lot of us. A Ducks Unlimited banquet was coming up, and he was in charge of soliciting gifts from local businesses to raise money for the Ducks.

First came little outdoor raffle items that would appeal to the folks that spend a lot of time in the woods. The idea was they would buy raffle tickets just for the fun of it. It also didn't hurt that pretty co-ed cheerleaders from Elon and the University at Chapel Hill were recruited to sell the tickets. This event raised a lot of money, but the most important part of the banquet was the auction. High dollar sporting items were designed to be auctioned at just the right time during the festivities when a couple of drinks and a first class dinner had loosened the purse strings of good old boys with money to burn. Coleman was in charge of getting all these gifts together. I don't think he even realized when he was doing it, but the major auction item, one that was designed to be the piece de resistance and would be presented at the end of the banquet, was an eight-week-old Black Labrador puppy. It just so happened this puppy had Dick Coleman's name on it.

As it turned out, Dick was the successful bidder for the puppy, and

Jim Lasley and I helped him get the little dog home after the successful banquet. The ducks would have a lot of money generated from the affair, and a bunch of dollars came from Dick when he couldn't resist bidding for what would become his lifelong dog friend.

The Lab, named Honcho, would grow into a hundred pound, wired tight, bird-retrieving machine and would influence several of us to get retrievers of our own. Jim was the first. Jim and I had just started a small weekly newspaper and spent a lot of time at the office getting the new enterprise up and running. Coleman's men's haberdashery was located around the corner, and Dick would usually stop by our little office on his way to work. Invariably, the conversation would center on how the training was going with his new puppy. Jim, a past bird dog owner, got the bug and with the help of Coleman found a breeder of golden retrievers. Before you knew it, he had a perky little blond puppy he named Sandy.

After a bit, along came Richard Cockman, an outdoor enthusiast whose father-in-law Curly Sanders owned several champion English Setters. In no time, Richard, an expert in his own right on blood lines of Labradors, had a couple of black Lab puppies of his own.

Then started the training. Alamance Wildlife Club was the perfect place, with a pond where the dogs could practice water retrieves and rolling fields for single marks and hand-signal training. Dog school was in session. For a while I just watched. I would ride to the club with the dog handlers and their charges, kick back and watch them as they went through their training routines. But me with a dog? No thanks, too much responsibility. That is until one day I realized how much fun the boys were having. Early one evening after an afternoon watching the handlers and dogs work, Linda and I were sitting on the patio talking about how they were progressing when she suggested that I get a retriever and join the fun. The very next day, Jim and I began the search for my puppy, and soon Paddle, a nine-week old yellow Lab fur ball, became part of our family. Other guys joined in on the fun, too. Tom Pate showed up at the Wildlife Club with a cute little Boykin Spaniel. In those days, Boykins had not been recognized by the American Kennel Club as a certified breed, so Princess, as she was named, couldn't participate in the field trials of the Tar Heel Retriever Club, to which most of us belonged. Made no difference though, the little dog ran in all the training tests and even showed up some of her bigger, more acceptable dog friends, or more acceptable to that pious group, the AKC. We enjoyed working with all breeds of dogs, and Pate later got a big rangy black Lab he named Gilly, so he could make the road trips to the many field trials the Tar Heel Club hosted. We made friends across the state. Dogs and handlers have a lot in common; and from mill owners to blue-collar laborers, everybody was treated the same. When you and your dog are on the line with a double mark and blind retrieve, the only thing that makes any difference is the dog. Everybody is equal; that is until after the test. Then come bragging rights.

The Tar Heel Club sponsored some marvelous field trials. One I remember above the rest was a spring weekend in Siler City at the farm of our good friend, Edwin Clapp. Edwin's dog, a big leggy yellow Lab, was one of the top dogs in our group. I remember dove hunting with them early one season when his dog, Dick (no relation to Coleman) jumped a five-foot cattle fence to retrieve a downed dove. At the trial on Edwin's farm, my little three-month-old Lab placed first in the puppy stakes.

Before it was over, almost every one of my bird hunting friends had retrievers of some breed. Bryan Pennington, a good duck-hunting buddy, had a little wirehaired pointing Griffon named Shug, that would retrieve anything from a duck to a squirrel. She would even go out to her kennel and retrieve her dog bowl when it was time for supper. These special dogs during that special time helped us become the individuals we are today. They were like family and were treated as such, and I know that I'm a better person because of the furry companions who shared my life.

Coleman, the boy who started it all, said it best as we sat on the tailgate of his Blazer late one afternoon after a successful dove hunt. The dogs were under the truck cooling down and resting. A beautiful early fall sunset was sinking behind the tree line to the west.

"Bryant," he said as we watched the afternoon come to an end. "You reckon dogs go to Heaven when they die?"

"I don't know," I replied. "Seems like I've read somewhere that there is a religious group that believes animals don't have souls."

"Well," Coleman said, matter-of-factly as he stood up and stretched. "If they don't go, I don't want to go either."

Nature's Light Show

"March," the Old Man said, "is a fine month for remembering. I suppose that's because there is really nothing else you can do in it. Don't ever let anybody tell you that getting old happens in the autumn of your life. It happens in March." Robert Ruark - The Old Man and the Boy

March was a couple of weeks away. I was up in the "roost", an apartment over my garage where I hang out, read, write when the muse strikes, clean shotguns and hunting gear, and think about weighty things such as where to go on my next sporting foray. It was raining outside, a cold, steel gray rain that threatened to turn into snow anytime. I had just gotten home from the last duck hunt of the season and had gear strung all over the place, most of it muddy and damp. It had been a good hunt. A hunt that would go into the journal with four stars. The kind of hunt I would remember, embellish, and talk about for years to come. My mother always told me that everyday should be lived to the fullest because you need to have those memories to tide you over in your golden years. I like to think that these past days afield are stocking my mental library, even though I'm nowhere near my golden years. Silver, maybe.

Tall pines outside the roost windows were swinging back and forth in the rain and wind. The old dog kennel where Mackie, my last yellow lab and hunting companion, had lived was forlorn and lonesome. Her doghouse just as it was the day she left us. Mackie died two years ago after a grand life, and I couldn't yet make myself find a replacement. Whoa, I thought. Time to go to the mental library and pull out some good memories to get me away from this melancholy. I went over to the bar, poured three fingers of good scotch that I keep for just such occasions and settled in the old lounge chair that's right beside a bookcase full of my favorite outdoor authors.

I went to my own mental Dewey decimal system, looked under D for dogs and pulled out a dusty memory that I hadn't thought about in years.

Paddle, my first lab, was nine weeks old and on the way from Pennsylvania aboard Piedmont Airlines flight 301, due to land anytime. I was at the freight office where airline freight was picked up. The attendant told me that the plane was on time, and if I wanted, I could step out on the loading dock and watch for it. Times have changed, haven't they? Sure enough, the big jet taxied to the passenger terminal and began unloading. A tractor pulling carts loaded with freight headed toward the dock but stopped about 40 yards short to wait its time to unload. The driver walked purposely toward the building. When he came up the steps, I asked him, "You don't have a little lab puppy in with those bags do you?"

"Why, I sure do. Cute little thing. Walk on out there and look. We'll have everything unloaded in a few minutes."

I went down the steps to the line of freight carts, saw a little dog travel cage and looked inside. In the back corner sat a little yellow puppy. She looked at me and yawned. That day began a relationship that would last fourteen years.

Wind was picking up outside the roost, and rain rattled the windowpanes. Almost sounds like sleet, I said to myself as I filed that long-ago memory back in its spot and pulled out another.

It was early afternoon at Hyco Lake in the northern stretches of Person County. Paddle and I were launching my little widgeon duck boat at the landing on the western side of the lake. We were planning to hunt until dark and then meet up with my old hunting partner, Bubba, at his cabin on the south side of the lake. Bubba's cabin sits high on a cliff overlooking the headwaters with his boathouse at the bottom of a long set of steps. I was going to motor up to the boathouse after the hunt. Bubba was tied up that afternoon, and we planned to hunt together the next morning. I hadn't counted on ice. My little duck boat is about 10 feet long with a wide beam. She's decked over with a cockpit big enough for Paddle, a dozen or so decoys and me. She's rated for a ten-horse kicker, but I had a seven and a half Mercury on her that would push the little boat as fast as I wanted to go. It takes a while to get her on plane, but once you do, look out.

Earlier in the season, Bubba and I had discovered a cove that black ducks loved way back close to the power plant. To get to it, we had to go under a cable that the power people had put up and then through a small canal for about 200 yards opening into a little undisturbed lake. Ducks often used it as a resting area. It became our honey hole and was my destination for the day's hunt. The weather had been unusually cold, but water discharged from the power plant usually kept the deep-water lake open. So as I motored toward our hunting spot, ice was the furthest thing from my mind. I was going to hunt until about dark and then scoot on up to Bubba's place.

As I rounded the last bend before the cut that ran into our spot, I hit skim ice that immediately got thicker. No way I'm gonna get through here, I thought, and reverted to plan B. Plan B was to hunt as close to the area as possible, so I pulled into a small cove, put out the decoys and covered us with a camouflage tarp. The little widgeon has a low profile almost like a layout boat, so Paddle and I would just hunt out of her. It was a slow afternoon with only a couple of bufflehead ducks working our rig; and remembering that I would have to go back to the landing, load up and drive to the cabin, I decided to pick up the dekes early.

It was cold. My little thermometer that I keep in the shell box read

18 degrees. Paddle and I were glad to head back to some warmth. We got the little boat up on plane, and I hunkered down behind Paddle to dodge some of the spray that was freezing on the boat and us. When I made the turn west into the big part of the lake, I motored down to cut back on the spray.

We were now pretty well iced over and, at this speed, had another 40 minutes before reaching the landing. A majestic sun was sinking into the west in a blaze of all its glory. The colors were almost a purple gold reflecting in a fiery path across the lake.

I noticed that Paddle kept looking back to the stern, and I thought she was just dodging the spray until I glanced around and saw a full moon rising from the east. The silvery white path reflected from the moon across the lake merged with that from the sun, and we were center stage, lit up by nature's own light show. I was so caught up by the sight that I cut the kicker, and Paddle and I drifted along watching God's handiwork in all its magnificent beauty. It lasted only a few minutes and was gone.

We made it to the landing about dark.

Well, I thought, time to quit this reverie and clean up some of this duck hunting gear. It's not going to get put up by itself. And hey, it's not March yet. I've still got two more weeks of quail season left. I wonder if Joe would let me walk over the old dove field down on his farm? Might jump a covey. Hmm, think I'll give him a call.

The Winter Storm

It was going to snow! Early that morning when I stepped out the back door to our patio I could smell it in the air. The sky was slate gray. High cirrus clouds were moving slowly from the northwest. It was eerily quiet, and the birds, unusually subdued, looked as if they were wearing down-filled coats with all their feathers puffed up to keep warm. Our birdbath was skimmed over with ice, and I broke it up with a stick and made a mental note to get warm water to refill it. Yes sir, I said to myself, it's gonna snow before lunch.

I went back inside to confirm my prediction with TV's Channel 2 and Lee Kinard and his morning show. In those days before cable TV, there were, at the most, maybe three channels available to TV watchers. We had an antenna fastened to our chimney with a rotor that would turn it in the direction of the station. Most of the time, we watched the Greensboro channel and tuned in to get the weather and news in the morning before heading out to work. I, along with my business partner, had a fledgling newspaper up and running. Linda, my bride, was teaching second grade. Tommy, our son, was in the first grade; so when something like a potential snowstorm was on the horizon, things around our household became a little jumpy.

"School's been cancelled!" Linda exclaimed as I walked back into the kitchen.

Tommy was eating his breakfast saying, "I want to build a snowman!"

Immediately Linda's survival instinct kicked in. "We need to go to the grocery store for more supplies."

"Okay," I replied. "You get ready, I'll take Tommy with me. We'll let Paddle out to run and then we'll go to the store."

Paddle, my new yellow lab, was just growing out of puppyhood and was raring to go. She romped around the backyard then ran to the back of the Bronco wanting to load up and go play.

"No girl, maybe later," I said as I put her back in her kennel.

She whimpered showing her disappointment. Linda came out the back door. "Are you ready? The TV said snow should start falling before lunch."

"Let's ride before they sell all the milk," I replied.

Linda laughed as we climbed in the Bronco and headed to Winn-Dixie. The place was packed with happy shoppers anticipating the winter storm. We loaded up with all kinds of goodies and drove home.

"Perfect timing. We can put up the tree this afternoon."

Christmas was two weeks away and we had been planning to decorate the tree over the weekend, but now with school canceled, we had an unanticipated extra day.

In short order, I brought the tree in from outside and placed it in the stand in a corner away from the fireplace. We had bought it on Monday, a freshly cut Frasier fir, and it smelled great. I then went back outside to our stack of wood and got an armload. We'd have to have a fire later that afternoon.

The sky seemed to be getting darker with lower, angry looking clouds moving across the horizon. Paddle started barking in her kennel. "No barking," I called, and she went back in her doghouse. It's a good thing I had bought more cedar bedding for her. She should be plenty comfy if it does snow. Maybe we'll go down to the duck hole after lunch. The duck hole was what I had named a little creek where I hunted wood ducks and mallards during the season. The little stream proved to be very productive in the duck-hunting department and was a great place to train her as a little puppy. She had been with me several times before the season opened and retrieved dummies thrown across the creek, but she had yet to retrieve a duck. Maybe before the season is over, I thought. Back inside, Linda was making sandwiches for lunch.

"I'm going to the office to check on things and then out to the duck hole with Paddle to let her run a little bit," I said. "I'll even take my shotgun in case I'm attacked by a crazy mallard."

Linda laughed, "This is supposed to be a heavy snow. Don't you get out there and get stranded."

"Nah, I'll take a couple of sandwiches with me, eat lunch at the creek and be back before the first flake falls."

Everything was okay at the office. We were lucky that the snow was coming on a Friday, which gave us the weekend to get back to normal, hopefully. Paddle was wired tight as I pulled up to the gate to the pasture that we had to cross on the way to our little duck preserve.

"Hang on, girl. I'll let you out in a minute and you can go play."

I parked the Bronco back in the stand of trees bordering the creek feeding into the big lake that was a water impoundment for the city. Paddle and I usually stayed away from the lake, concentrating on the creek for our efforts. It was getting colder, and I saw that the water bordering the bank was covered in skim ice.

I took my shotgun out of the case and told Paddle, "Okay, girl, go run." She jumped out and raced to the creek, broke the skim ice, got wet and ran back to me as if to ask, "Why is the water hard?" Sleet began to bounce off the truck.

"We don't have a lot of time, girl. Go play."

I walked through the tree line and followed Paddle as she edged toward the big water. I whistled to her, and as she was loping back to me, a duck came flying down the creek toward the lake. I snapped off a shot, and the duck crumpled and hit the ice about fifty yards from the bank. Paddle was off like a bullet, and all my whistling did no good in turning her. She was on a mission. Breaking the ice out to where the duck had landed, Paddle began quartering in a circle. Unfortunately, when the duck came down, the force of the fall knocked it under the ice and it couldn't be seen. Paddle kept at it until the bird popped up right in front of her. She grabbed it, swam back, walked up on the bank and presented me with the biggest black duck I'd ever seen. I couldn't believe it. Paddle's first duck retrieve, and it was one that I would remember forever. No big deal for her, though.

She shook freezing ice from her coat and looked up at me as if to say, "Okay, boss, what's next?"

Snow began to fall in earnest, and I decided we'd better get on home. Paddle settled down in her spot in the back, and I put the Bronco in four-wheel drive. The snow was getting deep fast. We were dripping wet from the sleet, snow, and creek water but the heater from the little Bronco soon had us warm. It was a great ride. Christmas carols were playing on the radio, and I sang along when Bing Crosby came on with his famous "White Christmas." Paddle dozed and didn't budge when I had to stop a time or two to clean the frozen windscreen. She was content in her favorite place.

Later that evening after Linda and Tommy had gone to bed and I was closing up the house, I sat down in front of the dying fire and thought back to how much fun everyone had had today with our first winter storm of the season. Tommy got to build his snowman, Linda made one of her favorite pound cakes, and Paddle retrieved her first duck and was sleeping on her special rug beside the fireplace as content as only a hunting dog can be after a day afield.

And me? I thought, "What the heck?" I went over to my little den bar, poured three fingers of a single malt Scotch I was saving for a special occasion, and put another log on the fire. I can't think of many occasions that will get more special than this.

Just a Couple of Snow Dogs

It was an exciting time, ten days before Christmas, the weather getting ready to break, duck season at its height and me with a little time off to enjoy the fun. Paddle, my yellow lab, and I were in our backyard around dusk loading up the old Bronco with all the paraphernalia that it takes for a successful duck hunt. Most of the early part of the season had been quite mild, therefore not much success in the duck department. We hoped that the weather report would be dead on for our before-daylight rendezvous with Haw River ducks. It sure felt like it.

"Look at that ring around the moon, Paddle."

A waning full moon hung low in the sky, and wind blew in gusts out of the northwest. Leaves in our big white oak tree rustled ominously. The giant old oak refused to give up her leaves without a struggle. She was always the last to present barren branches to a winter sky. I hoisted the Grumman canoe on top of the Bronco and tied her down. In the early fall, I had camouflaged the boat with marsh brown and flat black paint. She looks pretty good, I thought as I grabbed a sack of decoys out of the shed. I only planned to take eleven. You never put out an even number in a decoy spread. Bad luck, the old-timers say; and river hunting doesn't require many decoys.

Paddle didn't want to get back in her kennel. She was ready to hunt. "All right, girl. Morning will be here before you know it. Tell you what, how about a biscuit and some fresh bedding for your house, then sack time."

I poured a whole bag of cedar shavings in Paddle's doghouse, gave her two dog biscuits and said goodnight. Wind was still blowing strong out of the northwest and clouds scudded across the moon. It's gonna be a great day tomorrow, I thought as I went in to fry up some fresh country sausage for biscuits in the blind.

Linda, my bride, had the sausage already sizzling when I walked in shivering. "Man, it's getting cold out there. It ought to be an interesting morning."

"You're crazy, you know. The weatherman just predicted a big snow for the weekend, supposedly arriving some time tomorrow. I don't like you out in that weather alone. Suppose something happened?"

"Hey, Paddle will be with me," I laughed. "Don't worry, we're just gonna be on the river, you know up where John and I built the blind late last summer." John H. and I had hauled a bunch of plywood and surplus lumber that we scrounged from here and there and built a box blind on the southern point of a little island in the middle of the river. It was pretty well constructed, and we hoped to get a lot of shooting out of it.

The Haw River meanders slowly through farmland from Swepsonville to Saxapahaw. It flows into a small lake built by a long ago out of business textile company. The old dam still backs up quite a bit of water, and we discovered a couple winters ago that the shallow lake was a great resting area for ducks moving south.

I've always had a hard time sleeping before a duck hunt, and this one was no different. It seemed as if every hour, I'd check the clock. And when I heard a little sleet rattling on the windows about 3:30, I decided to get the show on the road. I had my hunting clothes laid out and had slept in the guest room so my early morning wouldn't wake Linda. In ten minutes, I was down stairs with the coffee cooking. I warmed up the sausage biscuits and stuffed them in my gunning bag, leaving one out for Paddle and me to munch on the ride to the scout hut where we would launch the canoe. I stepped out the back door and squinted into a fine sleet that blew across the yard at a slant. Our outdoor thermometer that hung on Paddle's kennel read 20 degrees. Paddle was watching me all the while with her head stuck out her doghouse wondering if we really were going out in this stuff.

"Come on girl, get in the truck. We're gonna have a big time this morning." I fired up the old Bronco, letting her warm up while I scraped ice off the windscreen. Paddle watched me from her customary passenger seat. My hunting partners always said that she looked as if she could drive if I let her. I climbed in and headed out the driveway. Sleet seemed to be falling faster.

The drive out into the country was like riding in a Hallmark Christmas card. Lights from Christmas trees, combined with city street decorations, made for a memorable ride. I couldn't drive very fast and was glad that I had allowed more time to get to the cut for the scout hut.

We've always called the derelict, run-down building on the bank of the Haw the scout hut. At one time, it was supposedly the meeting place for youngsters from the country surrounding Saxapahaw, but now it was just a broken down memory of more prosperous times. For me, though, it made a great place to park and gave me access directly to a steep bank to the river. A gravel road ran from the highway to a couple ruts that were really more like a firebreak, which angled down a steep hill to the clearing of the hut. Not many people made it that far, so it was perfect for me.

We stopped at the cut at the end of the gravel road, and I put the old truck in 4-wheel drive. Sleet, which seemed to be coming down at a faster pace, was so cold it was like dry sand and really presented no problem as far as traction was concerned. Next stop Haw River, I thought as we eased down the road.

Visibility was close as I spotted the remains of the little building and pulled the truck as near the bluff overlooking the river as I could. "Okay,

Paddle, let's get started."

While Paddle checked out all the bushes, I got the canoe down and loaded in record time. Sliding it down to the river was easy; getting it back up might be a different story, I thought as I hooked up the electric motor. As cold as it is, I hope the battery holds. I whistled Paddle into the bow of the canoe and pushed off upstream. The sleet changed to snow.

Heavy snow on a slow flowing river during the dead of night is almost surreal. It's as if you're floating with no real contact with the water. Ambient light only emphasizes the blackness. Every now and then, I'd flick on my flashlight, which did absolutely no good. Paddle looked as if she had turned into a snow dog, but she sat quietly in the bow watching the river. It was almost a whiteout. I could only tell that I was still heading upstream.

Paddle started whining just before I ran dead on into the box blind. I shut down the electric motor, grabbed a canoe paddle and put out the decoys. "Lotta good they'll do, I thought. They'll turn into snow ducks in a minute. After hiding the canoe on the little island, we settled down to wait for the dawn. It was snowing harder.

A gray morning slowly materialized out of the cold as the wind picked up. There were breaks in the swirls of driven snow blowing across the river, and I could almost see to the eastern bank. Paddle sat on her step outside the blind, ever vigilant for a duck. I grabbed my thermos, poured a cup of hot coffee, unwrapped a still warm biscuit and leaned back on the bench that John and I had built that summer. No self-respecting duck is gonna be flying in this weather, I thought. About that time three great big greenhead mallards buzzed the blind almost knocking my hat off. Paddle looked up at me as if to say, "What are you doing in there?" I hadn't even loaded my shotgun.

The next hour was fast and furious. Ducks in groups of five to twenty sailed down from the sky right toward us. Evidently, we had struck the mother lode. Our timing was perfect. I believe the ducks could have cared less, though, about the decoys that now looked like snow geese. They were just looking for a place to get out of the weather.

I shot well, and Paddle retrieved every duck as we filled our limit. Snow was now gusting intermittently, looking as if it might stop for a while. My sausage biscuit and now cold coffee sat on the bench undisturbed. I'll just wait until we get to the truck, I thought as we loaded the boat, picked up decoys and headed through a silent frozen winter scene to the landing.

Cold hastened our loading of all the gear in the truck, and I quickly got in the old Bronco to warm me up as well as Paddle. She was curled up on the seat smelling of fresh cedar. A tired, happy dog. I poured some much needed coffee and just sat there for a bit savoring the moment. Paddle looked up me and I scratched her ears.

"What do you think, Paddle? A good day, huh? Santa Claus sure came to see us a little early this year."

I put the truck in gear and headed up the cut. It started snowing again.

The Cypress Swamp

Merchants Millpond hunkers down in Gates County on the far northeast corner of North Carolina. It's a buster to get to, but as four of us found out in the late eighties, it's well worth the trip. We were into canoe paddling in those days, and most weekends would find us on a stretch of water, slowly drifting a laid-back swamp or black water river.

That is, if we weren't riding a roller coaster of a white water rapid. I believe it was my good friend John Vernon who actually put us onto Merchants Millpond and Bennetts Creek.

John did quite a bit of bird hunting in those days, and Gates County was one of his favorite places to hunt and one of the few locations that supported a growing population of the noble Bobwhite. I wish it were so today, but I understand that the county, like most everywhere else in the state, has also suffered from a demise of the little birds, much to the misfortune of bird hunters.

It was late winter, and spring seemed to be forever away. Duck season was over and it was too cold to fish, except for the diehards, and we weren't in that group by any means. We were sitting as close to a blazing fire in the fireplace at the old Alamance Wildlife Club as we could get. Dick Coleman, one of the ringleaders of our group and major proponent of road trips, threw another log on the fire.

"I'm bored stiff. We need to go somewhere and do something. Sitting around this fire is making me old."

That's when Vernon tossed in the idea of canoeing Merchants Millpond. "I was in Gates County last fall, bird hunting with some of my good lawyer friends."

"Let me stop you right there," threw in Coleman. "Is there such a thing as a good lawyer?"

Coleman and Vernon were always at it in a friendly way, Coleman being an arch conservative and Vernon leaning a little to the left. We always had some good conversations out of that pair. "If my good friend from the right would listen for just a second, even he will be enlightened," responded Vernon.

This is going to be good, I thought as I walked over to the fridge to get a beer. "Can I get anybody anything?"

"How about getting Coleman an open mind," Vernon replied.

"It looks as if I'm gonna have to call in the heavy guns. What's Bobo doing today?" Coleman said laughing. Tom Bobo was also a member of the group, and if it was possible, even a little more to the right of Coleman. I lined up with Coleman and Bobo; but Jim Lasley, a newspaperman, also more of the liberal kind, made the group even out, politically that is. We always had some great talks, and I think our differences made us even stronger friends.

"Before I was so rudely interrupted and as I was saying," laughed Vernon, "Merchants Millpond up in Gates County is something to see. It's one of the largest pure Cypress Swamps in the state, and if we really want to make a trip out of it, we could also paddle Bennetts Creek. The creek flows south out of the Millpond into the Chowan River. Probably take us three or four days, enough to keep even Coleman interested."

"Okay," Coleman replied, fired up now that a road trip was in the air. "When do we leave?" As we later found out, a man by the name of A. B. Coleman, no relation to our good friend Dick, purchased the Millpond in the sixties and later donated it to the state. That gift, along with land the Nature Conservancy contributed, now makes up the 3,250 acres of Merchants Millpond State Park.

We left home base late on a Friday, and the six-hour ride put us there after sundown. I've always hated to pitch camp after dark, and this trip was no exception. We kind of felt our way into the boat landing area of the millpond and put up tents right behind the vehicles. After a scratch supper of sardine sandwiches, we piled into the tents, hoping to get an early start the next morning. Sometime during the night, I thought I heard a bobcat cry, but I went right back to sleep.

I was the first up the next morning right before sunrise. A cool thick fog, almost heavy enough to be rain, floated out of the swamp. Cypress trees stretched heavenward, their top branches obscured by the mist. Coleman came yawning out of his tent, and we stood soaking up the silence. Somewhere deep across the waters of the millpond, we heard a loud splash along with the hacking croak made by a blue heron. "I've read," Coleman said, "that this area is the northern most extent of alligators' habitat. You reckon that's what we just heard?"

"Nah," I replied, "it's too cold for alligators up here. If they're up here, they're still hibernating or whatever it is they do in the winter."

"Yeah, you're probably right. Let's get a move on. We've still got to take one of these cars down to the Chowan where we'll take out. We're burning daylight."

John and Jim were up by then, and we left them to pack the canoes while Coleman and I made the car portage. We arrived back at the millpond a little before noon and debated on camping another night at our present campsite or heading on down the creek after a brief paddle around the swamp. We decided to hit the creek. The headwaters of Bennetts Creek are on the western side of the Great Dismal Swamp, and the creek flows into and out of Merchants Millpond State Park. South of the millpond, the creek meanders through the Chowan Swamp and into the Chowan River, our ultimate destination.

Jim and John had packed the canoes perfectly, but unfortunately, after our brief tour around the swamp, we had to unpack them again so we could portage them over the dam that held back the waters of the millpond. Even with the late start and difficulties faced in crossing a couple of beaver dams, we still made it several miles down the creek before stopping to camp for the night.

The rest of the trip was exactly as we had pictured it with abundant wildlife and waterfowl. We had great meals cooked by John, our executive outdoor chef, and were constantly amused by the dry wit of Dick Coleman. Our easy float ended after three days when we emerged from the little creek into the immense Chowan River.

It's been years since our adventure in Gates County, but I hope to make the same trip again this fall. I understand that a group of volunteers by the name of the Stewards of Bennetts Creek has constructed steps and a dock on the creek side of the millpond. It'll be interesting to see if they have made the right kind of progress on that little creek that flows so delicately into the mighty Chowan.

Beloved Season, Remembered Friend

When the summer sun meets her solstice and the earth begins to meander on back south toward the fall equinox, bird hunters and bird dogs begin to get a little lift in their stride. It still might be 98 degrees in the shade with the long dog days of August still ahead, but the afternoon shadows are a little longer, cicadas are noisier, and dogs are digging for cool spots in the flower garden less often.

Opening day of dove season can be counted in days, not weeks anymore. Doves sitting on wires and flying over fields promote population reports among fellow hunters, and plans are laid as to where the best fields might be, who is going to have the best hunt, and how you can wrangle an invitation.

A cross between a southern family reunion and a small war, opening day of dove season is an event without equal and is mostly peculiar to the south. It's an exciting time and one that I've participated in as far back as I can remember.

Early in my hunting career, I learned that it's the trip and not the destination that counts. Preparation is everything; and great memories are made, most of the time, in getting ready for the hunt, not necessarily the hunt itself. The other evening as I was sitting in the swing on our side porch watching a full moon slowly rise and listening to the birds as they shut down for the day, I thought back to some of my hunts from the past and the great times, better yet, the great people I had the opportunity to meet. There was one gentleman that I only knew for maybe an hour or so; still, every time dove season rolls around, I think of him.

I met Hank about eight or ten years ago in the most unusual manner. I remember it was late August during a smoking hot summer, and I was on the way to my newly leased dove field to put up some no trespassing signs, not to keep people out, but to let other hunters know that I was going to be in the area. I had to make a couple of trips because, as usual, I forgot one thing or another.

The field is located on the south side of Pinebluff about twenty minutes from my house. On the first excursion, I noticed an older man walking on the side of the road just south of Aberdeen. He was hitchhiking, carrying a hand-lettered sign that read, "Heading south, no hurry."

Now I normally don't pick up hitchhikers, but the sign caught my attention, mainly because, as a college student, I did a lot of thumbing back and forth to school. In those days, it was an acceptable way of traveling, and a lot of young people used the old thumb as a means of acquiring transportation. I used hand-lettered signs myself as a tool to catch rides.

I grinned as I passed the old gentleman and thought he needed to be more specific as to his destination. I later found that he was as specific as he wanted to be.

On my second trip to the dove field, I noticed that the hitchhiker had not made a lot of progress. As the sun was kicking into second gear and it was really getting hot, I decided to stop and give the old fellow a ride. It turned out that the next thirty or forty minutes would make a huge impression on me as to the nature of the human spirit. I found that Henry, or Hank as he requested that I call him ("All my friends call me Hank."), was not living on the public dole, as I had imagined, but was traveling as simply as he could to see and understand how the rest of the country lived.

Hank was of an indeterminate age. He could have been anywhere from 50 to 70 years old, I couldn't tell. He was dressed in old but clean clothes and, besides his sign, he carried a small pack.

When I asked where he was heading, I learned his story. Hank had been a responsible husband and father. He had been a stockbroker by profession and had acquired what most of us would think of as the American dream. Hank had owned a large home in a country club area, had been a leader in the community, and was well respected by his peers. A perfect citizen. Then the unthinkable happened. His wife of more than thirty years was stricken with cancer and suddenly died.

As Hank put it, "I didn't know what to do. The children were grown and out on their own, and I was living a life that had no meaning. Jane was the world to me."

So Hank did what most of us would do, and that was to lose himself in his job.

"It was meaningless. I had all the money I could ever spend. I was living by rote. And then one morning it came to me. I was looking out the breakfast room window at a beautiful sunrise when I wondered how that sunrise would look in Montana."

By this time, I was enthralled with this old gentleman as he continued his fascinating story.

"I gave everything to the kids, sold the house and have been checking out sunrises across the country for the last four years. Now I'm on the way to Florida to visit my sister or maybe to Texas. That's a pretty part of the country in the early fall. I prefer hitchhiking when I can because I get to meet nice people like you."

I dropped Hank off at the racetrack close to Rockingham, gave him a bottle of water from my cooler and a business card and asked him to stay in touch. I didn't hear from Hank for a couple of years and he became a pleasant memory. Then one evening, my phone rang.

I was putting in extra time at the office trying to catch up on several projects that had been put on the back burner after the disastrous 9-11 terrorist attacks. Needless to say, the country was in turmoil. The phone call was from Hank. He was in Texas working at an elementary school as a custodian. To this day, I don't know why he called at that time. He said he just wanted to reassure me that the country was in great shape and our people would recover and persevere. We had a long and, for me, insightful conversation.

That was a while back and the last time I heard from him. A lot of water has flowed under the bridge since then. I've retired from my regular job, and Hank has probably moved on to greener pastures. But every year at this special time, I remember Hank's eyes as he looked at me and asked how dove hunting was shaping up.

"One thing I miss since I've been on the road, Tom, is our annual dove hunts back home. I envy you and hope you have a great season."

Somewhere, I'm sure, Hank is watching the same moonrise and, like me, preparing for a great opening day.

Maggie, We'll Miss You

Most of my hunting partners of the last fifty years will tell you that I'm a dog man. Not just a dog man, but a yellow Labrador retriever, duck hunting dog man. There have been very few years of my life when I didn't have a loyal canine companion, beginning in the second grade when my dad surprised me with a Curly Coated Retriever that I named Smut.

Smut was a member of the family until he passed away at the ripe old age of fourteen. I was in college when he left us, and that lead to my longest period without a dog until Paddle came along. Paddle was a yellow Lab with intelligence that amazed my hunting partners and me. There were some things that she accomplished in the field that someday I hope to write a book about, but this isn't a story about Paddle.

A couple years later, Mackie came to live with us. A yellow Lab hailing from southern Georgia, she fit right in with my family, and we wandered the woods and rivers for another fourteen years until she left me to my own pursuits. That was three years ago, and I still haven't made the effort to find just the right hunting partner to usher in my final years afield. I will, though. When the timing is right, I know there will be just the right little yellow Lab puppy waiting out there to amaze me again with her loyalty and ability.

But this isn't a story about a dog. Believe it or not, it's about a cat. A little calico ragamuffin thrown-away kind of a cat that we inherited when we moved to Southern Pines thirteen years ago. Her name was Maggie, and I buried her this morning before the remnants of hurricane Ida dumped tons of rain on us.

Now, I'm not a cat person, never have been, although I've always been around cats. I remember the cats on my grandfather's farm. They were my grandmother's, and there were always several around the premises. They even seemed to have specific duties. There were just regular yard cats, house cats, and barn cats required to keep the barn free of mice and other vermin. For their reward, they were fed all the milk they could drink and table scraps that the dogs didn't get. Grandmother kept two pans on the corner of the big wood cook stove, one for the bread she baked for the dogs and another for her cats. I remember the cats had names, and there always seemed to be a new litter of kittens roaming around all the time. These were working cats during a time in the South when animals pulled their weight.

Linda, my bride of forty plus years, is a cat person; and like me with my dogs, she has had feline companions her entire life. The day we moved into our home in Southern Pines, Linda got a call from the former owners. I was outside hauling boxes from here to yonder looking forward to a break from all of the moving hassle.

"Hey Tom," she called from the back porch. "The Samuels just phoned. They left one of their cats."

"They what?"

"Yeah, it seems that one of their cats is real skittish and almost man-shy. The moving people scared her, and they want us to try to catch her and they'll pick her up when they come back to Southern Pines next week." Yeah right, I thought. We've got ourselves a cat.

And try to catch her we did. Mr. Borrelli, our neighbor across the street, lent us a live trap.

"I know the cat," he said. "She's a little bit of a thing and as wild as they come.

Only Mr. and Mrs. Samuels can get close to her. I really believe she's been hiding in the culvert that goes under the street right over there." He pointed to the street corner near his yard.

"Well," I said. "I'll bait the trap and set it tonight and see if we can catch her. She's bound to be hungry." I put out the trap right before Linda and I went in for supper.

Later that evening when we were preparing for bed after a tiring day, Linda reminded me about it. "I'll check it in the morning," I sighed. "She'll be okay until then."

"Check it now. Something could get her in that thing. Come on, I'll go with you."

We walked out front near the post light where I had put the trap, and I could hear a hissing that sounded like a tire going flat, or worse scenario, a wild cat. "We've caught something and it's not happy. Don't mess with it and I'll get a flash light." The post light bulb had burned out, and all we could see was something black and mad in the trap. When I got back I stood at a safe distance and put the light on the trapped animal.

"Well, it's a cat, but it's not a sweet little thing like the Samuels said. I believe we've caught somebody else's tiger."

The cat's hair was standing straight up and under the flash, it looked solid black.

"Stand back, hon, and I'll release it. That can't be the cat we're after."

I stood sideways to the trap, opened the door, stepped back and watched as our escaped friend shot out like a cannon and ran straight to the culvert under the street.

"Oops, wrong. I believe that was our cat." Linda said nothing, just looked at me askance with her hands on her hips.

"Don't worry, babe," I said. "We caught her once, and we'll catch her once more."

Wrong again.

It took days of coaxing her closer to the house with cat food for her to finally end up in our backyard.

And that's how Maggie came to live with us for the next thirteen years. The Samuels gave up on trying to get her back, and over time Linda tamed the little kitty into becoming part of our family. She fit right in, made friends with Mackie, my dog, secured me as part of her staff, and in general, made herself known throughout the neighborhood. There is a time and season for all things. Maggie grew old, and in the past several weeks, began a decline that ended yesterday. In the afternoon, I noticed that she was asleep in the path leading down to my duck boats. For a couple of days previously, she had refused to eat and had become very weak. I walked down to her, knelt at her side, rubbed her head, and she meowed back as if to say everything was all right. I went on up to the roost, a small apartment over my garage, to finish working on a column. When I came back down stairs after an hour or so, Maggie was nowhere to be seen. I thought she'd likely gone back to the house, so I went up there to find her. She had disappeared.

Our backyard is fenced so there was no way she could have left the yard. I had always heard that a dying cat would seek a private place for its last hours, so I searched the backyard from top to bottom. Linda came out and I told her that Maggie was missing and we needed to find her because a storm was moving in that evening. We resumed our search. No luck. As we were standing near the woodpile, Linda thought she heard a soft meow. Maggie had crawled up under the tarp that I keep over the wood. She wasn't hiding, but that was going to be her last place.

Linda got Maggie's little cat bed, and I gently pulled her out from under the tarp and laid her in her bed. We put her in the garage realizing this would be her last evening with us. We went to bed, both of us silent with sad thoughts.

The next morning I got up early and decided not to wake Linda. The last chore in a pet's life with a family is not an easy one, and I wanted Linda to remember Maggie as she was the evening before, asleep in her little bed. In the garage sometime during the night, Maggie had a peaceful passing. I wrapped her in a towel and carried her back to the fence. She always loved to lie under a big pine close to the street and check out the passing cars. I quickly dug a grave, gently placed her in it and covered her. Rain started to sprinkle through the pines as I headed back to the house.

Maggie, We'll Miss You

Advice to A Young Hunter

It *had been a ho-hum kind of early duck season, so I decided to head home from our duck impoundments at Lake Mattamuskeet and catch up on some writing that I had delayed too long.* I usually do most of my creative stuff up in the Roost, the upstairs apartment above our garage. I can get out of my wife's way and away from distractions that might cause me to procrastinate the inevitable even longer.

While I was sitting at my desk, waiting for the elusive muse to strike, I decided to check the 384 emails I had received while pursuing the noble waterfowl. Most of my electronic mail concerns such fascinating items as where to vacation in the Russian steppes, or something even less important to me, and I usually delete them pretty quickly.

There was a message, though, from a young fellow that really got my attention. It went something like this: Mr. Bryant, My uncle took me duck hunting last winter out on the Chesapeake Bay. We were hunting with a guide who had all the gear so we were just participants. My question to you is since I plan to become a real duck hunter, what gear do I need to do an adequate job hunting waterfowl? I love your writing and read your columns every chance I get. Oh, by the way, I'm fourteen years old. Thanks for your help. Jack.

Hmmm, I thought. Smart kid with excellent taste. I'll see if I can't lend him a little of my expertise.

Jack, oh how I envy your early start in accumulating the necessary accouterments to make you a successful water fowler. You are entering an almost mystic endeavor which, I'm sure, during your lifetime will be obstructed by such things as work, money, and women. The lady you choose as a partner can overcome those temporary bumps in the road. I was fortunate in that my bride chose me and all my hunting paraphernalia and has overlooked my few misadventures in the field.

One such event occurred when I went wood duck hunting on opening day of the season. Unfortunately, that was the same Saturday we were moving to a bigger house and my mother, my son, and a good friend and his father were there to help Linda. I wasn't. Enough said about that. I don't want to open old wounds. After a few months, my bride forgave me and let me live to hunt another day.

Therefore, the single most important item you must consider when setting out on this noble adventure is the lady you will live with through many duck seasons. When you get closer to that magic day and are looking for a bride, I'll send you a form letter that a couple of buddies and I put together for a friend who was interested in a young lady from New York City. The letter included a little quiz about things concerning efforts in the field. For example, how long should it take you to clean a Canada goose? What's the best water repellent to use on your husband's boots? Easy questions like that. So what if it didn't work for Bob. I think it's a pretty good quiz and could help you later. Let me know when you need it.

Shotguns. I believe in your case, I would get a Remington 870 twenty gauge. This is a pump gun that chambers 2¾-inch as well as 3-inch ammunition. Of course, as you get older and more fluid in the money department, I would look at the autoloaders such as Browning, Winchester, and Remington. And you could always throw in a superposed Ruger. Remember, there is no such thing as too many shotguns.

Boats. I leave the big boats to friends, which brings another point. A good duck-hunting friend is hard to find. A good duck-hunting friend with a big boat is to be cultivated and cherished. I personally have a little Widgeon duck skiff with a 10-horse kicker for lakes and back waters, a 16-foot johnboat for rivers and bigger lakes, and a couple of canoes for jump shooting wood ducks on driftable rivers. Don't worry, the boats will come as you grow into the sport.

Decoys. Try to collect all the old L.L.Bean decoys you can find, not only great to hunt over, but as you get older, their presence will help you remember all the good times on those cold, snowy February and March days when the season is over. A good bet on utilitarian decoys would be the Green Head brand. I would get a dozen each of mallards and widgeons, a half dozen black ducks and a few teal. Decoys, like shotguns, will grow in number.

Duck calls. A duck call can be your best friend or your worst enemy. I've hunted with folks, not lately mind you, who would begin blowing a call the minute they were in the blind. These people should be avoided at all cost, primarily to save your hearing. Learning to blow a call takes time and practice, but be careful where you make the effort. When I first started blowing a call, a next-door neighbor thought a fox had gotten in her chicken coop. It caused quite a bit of consternation.

Retriever dogs. This will be the most important decision you make in your duck-hunting career. I highly recommend yellow Labradors, but that is just my personal preference. There are many good choices: Goldens, Labs, Spaniels. I even have a friend who duck hunts with an English setter, but that's a rarity. Also, very important to remember is that the cheapest money spent is on the purchase of a puppy. A good dog can teach a youngster a few tricks; but a bad dog, one without good genes, can only get worse.

Duck-hunting friends. I hope you will be as fortunate as I in acquiring good buddies to share fun with in the field. My hunting partners go back over thirty years, and we have shared many unforgettable experiences, some that haven't passed the statute of limitations, unfortunately, so enough said about that.

So, Jack, this should help you get started. Read all you can about the sport. The old timers like Havilah Babcock's *My Health Is Better In November*, Nash Buckingham's *De Shootinest Gent'man*, and the Bible for youngsters your age, Robert Ruark's *Old Man and the Boy*. These are books you will read and reread in your duck-hunting career; and hey, old Tom Bryant will even throw in an effort every now and then.

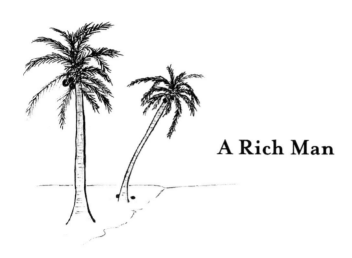

A Rich Man

"*Rich,*" *the old man said dreamily,* "*is not baying after what you can't have. Rich is having the time to do what you want to do. Rich is a little whiskey to drink and some food to eat and a roof over your head and a fish pole and a boat and a gun and a dollar for a box of shells. Rich is not owing any money to anybody, and not spending what you haven't got.*" Robert Ruark, The Old Man's Boy Grows Older

The only person I've known to come close to Ruark's description of a rich man was my grandfather. He came along at a time when hard work, a little luck, and a lot of smarts enabled him to accumulate wealth, but he knew how to use his money and his time.

I would say that I have been extremely lucky to follow along in my grandfather's footsteps, not so much with wealth, but now that I'm retired, with time. It has taken some adjustments, but Linda, my bride, and I, in the short years that we have been away from the everyday work hassle, have learned to slow down and smell the roses, or hunt ducks, or fish, or take camping trips, or just do whatever we want. I don't want to jinx our good fortune during these so-called golden years, but we're having a good time.

For the past several days, I've been sorting through and cleaning up duck hunting gear. After a duck season that will enter the hunting journal as a bust due to the spring-like weather, I've been anxious to begin our late winter adventure, which will be a fishing/camping trip down to Everglades City and Chokoloskee Island on the southwestern tip of Florida.

My grandfather introduced me to southern Florida when I was a youngster. He had a cabin on Halfway Creek, which flows out of the Everglades into Chokloskee Bay. During those days, I was fortunate that my grammar school principal let me take a couple weeks during the winter to visit my grandfather at his camp. I can remember him saying that the trip would be a great educational experience, and the only thing I would have to do would be write a paper about what I had learned and present it to my class when I returned.

For a twelve-year-old boy, the trip was quite an adventure. For eight days or more, my grandfather and I were out on the creeks and bays or roaming the 10,000 islands. We caught fish like you wouldn't believe. Snook, snapper, sheepshead, bream, trout, redfish, and an occasional channel bass. After a day on the water, we would come home with enough fish to feed half the neighborhood.

I had such a marvelous time during those visits that a few years ago on a trip to Key West, Linda and I decided to see if the area was the same as I remembered. In a way, I was reluctant to stop by Everglades City because I was afraid that it had gone the way of other early outdoor haunts of mine. Perhaps civilization had arrived and, in the name of progress, ruined everything. We were pleasantly relieved to see that it had changed very little. The coconut trees were fewer but still as tall and majestic as ever, and the old Rod and Gun Club was perched on the banks of the Barron River in all its remembered glory. Although we were there only part of a day, we resolved to add the location to our after-retirement plans and go back for a longer visit.

Two years ago we returned to the little village and spent a week at what Linda now refers to as "The Fish Camp." The little Airstream's campsite was smaller than we were used to, but its location was perfect, right on Chokoloskee Bay. We had all the conveniences of home with our little camper and beautiful views to boot.

Unfortunately on this trip, I was undersupplied in the fishing department. I reasoned when we left home that since we were going to be camping all around Florida, I wouldn't need much fishing gear. Wrong. On our next adventure, I hope to take my canoe and a couple bait casters and a fly rod. Last week I talked to the camp manager who told me an old line that I've heard before and wanted to be true. He said the fishing is so good that you have to hide your bait while you're baiting the hook or the fish will jump right in the boat.

I've always been interested in southern swamps, probably because I cut my teeth on black water rivers of South Carolina, again thanks to my grandfather. There are wild areas of beautiful primordial bog lands that can only be seen by small boats or canoes. I've paddled the Okefenokee Swamp on the border of Georgia and Florida several times; but in the past few years, it has turned into more of a tourist location, and Linda and I give it a wide berth. Man has succeeded in destroying a big portion of the Everglades by draining the northern area for cattle ranches and produce farms, but the lower section around Everglades City is holding its own.

Even though the community has been discovered by snowbirds (tourists from snow-bound states who head south for the winter), their numbers are not as many as in other areas of the state. The natives of the Everglades, including the Seminoles, have changed just as their counterparts have in other wilderness areas of the country. The old timers have died and the young generation is up to speed in everything, including electronics. When the feds took over the swamp in the early forties and made it a national park, some regulations took away the livelihoods of most of the local population. No more alligator hunting or trapping or commercial fishing and crabbing. So being an independent lot, the populace did what they had to do to make a living. Just like some of our

North Carolina mountain people, many of the folks surrounding the Everglades started making whiskey. When the federals found and destroyed their stills, they resorted to using their boats for smuggling drugs from South America. At one time, during a federal drug bust in Everglades City, a large part of the population was indicted.

Economically, the little town is different now for sure. Residents of Everglades City and Chokoloskee Island make their living by guiding fishermen and showing rich tourists around their incredible swamp. I like to think, though, that my visit means a little more than taking an airboat ride or participating in the newcomer tourist thing. On this adventure, I'll try hard to be recognized as a sportsman like my granddad and keep the Glades' interest at heart. Ruark was right. "Rich" is a state of mind. The older I get, the more I try to follow the Old Man's definition for what rich means to the outdoorsman. Watching a sunset over the 10,000 Islands doesn't cost a thing, but the reward is immeasurable. I know many folks with tons of money, big houses, fancy cars and all the fine wine and food they can eat or drink, but I'm afraid all that stuff may have kept them from seeing my kind of sunset.

The Old Man and the River

"And when he reached in that live well and pulled out that giant bass, I almost fell out o' the boat."

Linda looked at me smiling as she chopped up lettuce for our supper salad. We were camped in the little Airstream below Deland, Florida. I had just returned from a quick trip to Mother's old winter home in Astor on the St. Johns River. It's been years since anyone has used the old place, and I wanted to see what shape it was in. On this jaunt, I also checked out the Black Water Marina where my dad used to keep his little fishing skiff. Like everything else in Florida, it had changed. Not many boats, and the ones birthed there were giant party crafts supporting the rumor that the river has become more a cruising, sightseeing venue than a world-class bass-fishing location.

When I drove over to the public landing, I met an older fisherman just in from a day on the river, and that's when I saw the giant bass. The old guy had a boat from another era, and in the live well on his craft was the biggest bass I had ever seen. He told me about his catch and, surprisingly, invited me to go with him the next day. I was to call him around nine that evening to set up a time. My last fishing trip on the St. Johns was years ago, and I was wound tight with excitement. "Before you call, you might want to get your fishing stuff together and see if you need more equipment." Linda suggested.

Before we left home on this, our annual late spring camping and fishing trip, I had stored in the back of the Cruiser an ancient South Bend bait casting rod and reel that my grandfather had given me when I was a youngster and also my dad's old Garcia spinning outfit that my brother Guery had refurbished. I also put my aged tackle box in the storage trunk of the camper. Not the best fishing gear; it was more sentimental than practical.

"I'll wait," I replied. "Who knows, the fellow might back out since I'm a perfect stranger. He could've changed his mind. It's about nine. I'm gonna give him a call."

I went out under the awning of the Airstream where I could get better reception on the cell phone.

"Mr. Banks?" The phone was crackling a bit and I walked around to see if I could get a better connection.

"Yep, This is Jim Banks. What can I do for you?"

"Tom Bryant here, sir. I met you this afternoon at the boat landing in Astor. You were kind enough to offer to take me fishing tomorrow and wanted me to call at nine."

"Good for you, buddyroe. Meet me in the morning at the same place around five. Bring some cold drinks, if you want 'em, and a sandwich or two. We'll be gone about all day."

"What kind of fishing gear should I bring? Unfortunately, I only have a couple of ancient rods and reels."

"Sort of like us, old sport. They'll work fine. I've got plenty of fishing tackle and some rods if needed. See you in the morning."

I went back in the Airstream and relayed the conversation to Linda and she said, "You look like a kid the night before Christmas. Why don't you go on to bed? I'll fix some lunch for you to take, and I'll wrap up the rest of the pound cake which you can share with your new friend."

I knew I'd have a hard time getting to sleep. I was so antsy, sort of like the day before the opening of duck season. But it was really no problem, and it seemed as if I had just shut my eyes when the little alarm clock started its insistent ringing.

I arrived at the landing about four-thirty. Early as usual, I thought, but I had just parked the Cruiser in a slot close to the trees and grabbed my gear out of the back when I heard a motor on the river. I couldn't see the boat, but I recognized the unusual sound of the kicker from the afternoon before. There was a low fog across the black water, illuminated by a waning moon, and in a minute or two the pockety-pockety sound of the old engine came from around a far bend. A craft that looked like it had been built when my granddad was a youngster slid out of the mist like an apparition. Mr. Banks was amidships running the boat from what looked like a fiberglass center console, the only difference being it was made of wood.

"Put your gear aboard, sport. I'll hold her to the bank for you."

I tossed my fishing rods in the bow and we went putting and creaking, through swirling fog, heading upriver. There was a faint grayness coming from the east, promising a good day. I propped myself next to the console as Mr. Banks increased the speed of his boat and steered her toward the center of the flowing black water.

He leaned over and said in a loud voice, "We've got about a forty-minute run until we start fishing. You might want to sit up there in the bow. It'll be more comfortable." I moved to the forward bench and watched as the river flowed by. The early morning sun was beginning to shine through the trees throwing shadows from the bank. Every now and then, Mr. Banks would point out an alligator lying in the shallows.

In no time it seemed, the river opened into a large lake. "Lake George?" I shouted back at Mr. Banks.

"Yep. We'll be fishing in just a few minutes." He slowed the craft and turned toward a small opening that seemed to be a shallow creek flowing into the lake. It appeared to be impassable, and I was surprised when the narrow cut, bordered with live oaks covered with hanging moss, opened into a small lake. Banks shut the engine and let the boat drift.

He said in a low voice, "You better get your rig ready. Try not to bump the boat. This place holds some big bass and they oughta be hungry."

I unlimbered Dad's refurbished spinning outfit and was digging in my tackle box when Banks said softly, "Here, Bubba, try this lure. It's an old wooden topwater popper. Throw it at that cypress log hanging off the bank. Put it right where the log enters the water. I betcha there's a big un hanging out there."

The wooden lure had to be about as old as the boat, and I double-tied it to my twenty-pound test fishing line. Man, I thought, I hope I don't lose this thing.

My first cast was perfect. Almost bouncing off the log. I slowly reeled, the topwater lure making a popping noise. The lure was halfway back to the boat when an underwater object came after it pushing the water like a miniature submarine.

"Get ready!" Banks exclaimed. "That's a big un!"

The bass hit the bait like a freight train, and I reared back on the rod to set the hook. As the bass went deep, it was like I had caught a Volkswagen.

"Don't lose him!" Banks was shouting. "That bass could be a record breaker!"

I was trying to turn the fish back toward the boat and I kept hearing a persistent ringing noise. What is that sound? I wondered.

"Tom, Honey, its time to wake up, the alarm clock is ringing. Remember you're going fishing this morning and you don't want to be late."

A dream! I sat bleary-eyed on the side of the bed. The big fish was just a dream. But maybe not — the day's just starting.

Catching Up With Christmas

It seemed as if the Christmas season had sneaked up on me like a fox on a field mouse. Granted, the tree was already up and I planned to put the Polar Express electric train around the base as we had done the last couple of years, but something was just not right and I couldn't put my finger on it. Maybe it was the unseasonably warm weather or perhaps the lack of good old Christmas carols on the radio. Radio stations had been playing the same holiday music constantly since Thanksgiving, but too much of a good thing turns into too much of nothing. Something was amiss, and I just couldn't get the spirit.

I brought the train down from the closet in the attic and told Linda that I would lay out the track as soon as I got back from the dove field.

"You aren't going hunting today, are you? We have a ton of stuff to do before we go to South Carolina."

We were planning to go down to the farm to visit the family and see if there was anything we could do before Christmas week. The plan was to spend Christmas day with my 95-year young mother and my sister Bonnie. Since my brother Guery had built himself a house on the back pasture of the home place and he would celebrate with us, the holiday would really seem like a family reunion.

"No, I'm not going to hunt," I replied. "I'm going shoot some mistletoe from that big white oak growing beside the pond. You remember, the one I showed you last week."

Linda and I always go to the little farm I lease for dove hunting to clip greenery for decorations. On our venture to the woods the week before, I had spotted the mistletoe but didn't have my rifle on hand to shoot it out of the tree.

"Be careful and don't be late. We're having an early supper."

I flipped on the car radio for the ride to the dove field, but the same Christmas music was playing over and over again, so I put in a CD, Celine Dion's newest holiday effort. Her rendition of "Silent Night" was as pretty as I've ever heard. Just what I need, I thought, beautiful music and a trip to the woods. Finally, I'm catching up with Christmas. As I unlocked and opened the gate to the farm, I saw ten or fifteen Canada geese glide across the far end of the field. It looked as if they were dropping into the little pond bordered by the white oak harboring the mistletoe. Sorry, geese, I hate to disturb you but I need that mistletoe. And if you come back after Christmas, I'll be a welcoming party of one. It has been a while since I had a Christmas goose, and one would sure taste good around New Year's.

I pulled up to the little path that circled the pond and softly shut the door to the truck. As I eased around the far end, I saw the geese grouped under the big cypress that grows in about two feet of water. They saw me and began swimming hither and yon in confusion, reminding me of a Marx brothers' skit. Located where they were near the tree line, the only way they could get flying room was to head directly toward me, setting up a classic duck hunting, or in this case goose hunting, shot. They flew over my head honking like a bunch of taxi drivers in a Manhattan traffic jam.

I grinned as I threw up my imaginary shotgun and said, "Bam! Bang! Bam! Three geese in the pot."

The geese flew on complaining to each other about the interloper who disturbed their reverie. It was no problem shooting the mistletoe from the big white oak, and I got several clumps loaded with dainty, milk-white berries.

Back at the truck, I slipped on my coat. It's amazing how the temperature drops when the sun starts going down. The coolness reminded me of early season duck hunting at our lodge. This was the second year in a row that I had not been duck hunting.

Our group had dropped our lease on impoundments at Mattamuskeet, and unfortunately duck hunting in the Sandhills leaves something to be desired. But seeing those geese had brought back great memories of my times waterfowling. I opened the back gate to the Xterra and sat down as I would on the tailgate of a pickup, grabbed a drink out of the cooler and opened a pack of nabs for a little treat.

Clouds were drifting in from the west. Could be the weather was about to change. I used to watch the weather channel religiously first thing every morning, but it's not like it was in the early days. The folks running it now have turned it into something resembling reality TV, usually having some guy trying to survive, standing around in a hurricane or on the border of a tornado. Now my weather forecasting is to go outside, and if it's raining, I get some rain gear, if it's cold, a coat. It's a lot more fun having a little mystery in the atmosphere.

A couple of deer moved out into the field on the north side of the farm. They were as pretty as a picture as they browsed the grasses. Two more joined them as if they were going to have a regular party. I switched off the overhead lights in the vehicle and decided to watch for a while as two more young deer came out of the tree line to feed. A solitary red-tail hawk soared effortlessly over the fields, perhaps looking for supper.

Speaking of supper, time to go. I fired up the truck and watched as the deer moved back in the trees. On the way home, I thought about all the traditions our family has created in celebrating Christmas. I mentally made a list as I cruised through the country.

Number one would have to be the nine-foot Frasier fir that we always get directly from Ashe County and all the decorations we have accumulated over many years. And I love the aroma of the festive greenery placed throughout the house. Then there are the wonderful holiday foods including turkey, ducks and venison, and all the colorful desserts: Christmas cakes, pies, and cookies.

All this leads to the climax with the family gathering for our classic gift-giving on Christmas morning. Wonderful family traditions. But what made this Christmas even more special was my late afternoon trip to the peaceful, silent serenity of the woods. Deer grazing along the edge of the field, the geese on the pond, and the lone red-tail hawk, backlit by an early winter sunset.

It was as if Mother Nature had created a special Christmas card just for me.

Rocking Porch Resolutions

"January," Bubba said, "is named after the god Janus by the Romans for their ancient calendar. He was supposedly the god of beginnings or transitions. I'm probably telling you something you already know, though. Right, Coot?"

It was early January of a brand new year, and we were kicked back in a pair of rocking chairs in a sunny spot on the wraparound porch of Slim's country store enjoying the warmth of the mid-afternoon sun. Bubba had his legs stretched out and a steaming, freshly poured mug of hot coffee resting on the arm of his rocker. We had been in the woods early that morning squirrel hunting, a sport Bubba swears was relegated to the back corner by a bunch of yuppies who only enjoy the great outdoors so they can buy more spiffy clothes. I was halfway dozing and really didn't pay a lot of attention to what Bubba was saying. He was often coming up with some kind of off-the-wall information. He had bestowed the nickname Cooter on me years ago and it stuck.

"Seems like I remember some of that stuff, Bubba. Maybe that's why a lot of folks make New Year's resolutions. That's one type of new beginning, don't you think?"

"You're right," he replied. "But I think you and I fall into the category of transitions. We're too old for beginnings."

"Nope, speak for yourself. I don't consider myself old, maybe slowing down a little, but I can still do about as much as I could a few years back."

"You don't get it, Coot. I don't mean that we can't start a new beginning, but hey, I'm still working on some I started years ago. I just try to transition them every now and then. That way they feel like a new beginning."

"So you're saying some of the New Year's resolutions you made long ago have just transitioned into things you are doing today? I'm gonna think about that for a minute while I freshen up my coffee. You want some?"

"No, thanks, but you can bring me one of those ham biscuits that Leroy made this morning."

Leroy is Slim's cousin and worked for him part time. He now manages the ancient store that Bubba bought when Slim died. The old store didn't make too much money, but Bubba said it was a deal at any price. He needed a place to get away from too much civilization. It worked out well for both of them. Bubba had his place to go, and Leroy was familiar with the job.

I went in the store and said hey to a couple of the regulars who had just arrived. H.B. Johnson was dragging a slat-back chair from the corner to a spot in front of the woodstove.

"You and Bubba outside? I saw him when I drove up. He looked like a sleepy old hound dog resting in the sun."

"You're not far wrong, H.B. He sort of favors a few hound dogs that I'm familiar with."

The guys laughed, and I poured more coffee before going back outside.

"Take Falls Lake," Bubba said as I closed the side door and moved to my rocker. "We hunted there last week and it's nothing like what it was on our first visit, remember?"

Bubba was on a roll. When he gets on a topic, he chews it front ways, sideways, upside down and backward, like a bulldog with a new ham bone. "What's that got to do with resolutions?" I responded.

"Well, the first time we hunted there they had just finished the dam, and we were some of the first to try the spot for ducking. It turned out to be one of the best in the area. Then here came the troops, more duck hunters than you could shake a stick at. Soon the dam was closed, the lake filled, pleasure boaters came out all over the place, and duck hunting went south. Now that there aren't so many hunters, ducks have rediscovered the lake and hunting is getting better. You might say the place has transitioned and we have along with it, thus proving that old Janus wasn't far wrong."

"As old as we are, we could probably use that analogy in many of our hunting spots," I replied. "Take the Sartin farm, for example. Four hundred acres of some of the finest wild habitat in the whole county. Everything from ducks to turkeys and doves, deer and otter and beaver, even good fishing on the creek. All that is gone now, transitioned to ten-acre mini-farms owned by city folk who like to pretend they're farmers. No new beginnings there. In that case, our good place to hunt and enjoy nature was transitioned slam out o' business."

I could see Bubba literally chewing that over as he took a bite of his ham biscuit. "You've got a point there, Coot. I guess that situation goes with the territory of living a long time and watching the dubious benefits of progress. Sometimes I think maybe we were born a little too late. Another good example of how progress has done us in would be duck hunting at Currituck. Remember when we would go every winter to hunt with the Whitsons? I think that old crowd has died off, and the hunting is now so bad hardly anyone hunts there anymore. Another sign of growth and the 'benefits' of development."

Our conversation continued for a while until we decided to head home in time for our naps. I had a ways to drive, so I bade the boys inside goodbye and told Bubba that I'd give him a call later in the week so we could plan our hunt at Mattamuskeet.

On the way home, I mused over our talks about resolutions and New Years in general. Bubba and I have seen a bunch of Januarys roll around, and for better or worse, we've made the best of whatever came. We've still got our health; and in the woods, we're able to do about anything we want. As Bubba says, we've learned to walk around it rather than climb over. A certain amount of wisdom does come with age. I often wonder, though, what the next generation will experience. Will they be able to see Tundra Swans rafted up by the thousands on Lake Mattamuskeet, or even a wild squirrel scurrying around a giant oak as Bubba and I did that morning?

Time changes a bunch of stuff; and as the ancient Roman god Janus probably knew, not every new beginning is a good thing.

The Alaska Highway

As a youngster growing up in the low country of South Carolina, camping came early and easy for me. My first adventure was in the small backyard of our home. With equipment consisting of an old grey-green surplus army blanket for a tent and another for my bedroll, I was ready to begin what would become a life-long love of sleeping in the great outdoors. I remember my blanket tent draped over an arm of my swing set with a couple of bricks anchoring the corners. Needless to say, that first night's camp found me in the house not long after sunset. But it was the beginning, and I was off and running, sometimes literally, but in most cases camping for the next 60 years.

When I was the ripe old age of seven, my parents moved to Pinebluff, NC and camping experiences became more and more a way of life. As soon as school was out for the summer, my good buddies of Boy Scout Troop 206 and I would begin reconnoitering for the best camping areas in our surrounding territory. And our territory consisted of any likely spot from south of Aberdeen to just beyond the banks of Drowning Creek. We had a lot of room to pitch our tents.

As time went by, we became more knowledgeable of what we were doing, but our equipment remained the basic Uncle Sam's surplus. From two shelter halves put together to sleep under, a moldy tarp for ground cover and a bed roll of one, or if it was real cold, two wool army blankets, we were set for an adventure for a weekend or week, the longer the better. As I grew older, my camping became more sophisticated and camping places wide and varied. Most of the experiences were of my own choosing, but others were initiated by simply an urge to remain relatively healthy. There was the time on the raging Haw River when a good buddy of mine and I spent the evening on an island in the middle of the rising torrent while our canoe was wrapped around a couple of boulders under water. The little spit of land we were stranded on was about 5 feet wide by 20 feet long and promised to be submerged before dawn. But that's not the story I'm here to tell.

I've always longed to see the Canadian Yukon wilderness and Alaska, the last frontier, but having to work for a living and wanting to see the area from the ground up, as it were, I had to put that camping experience on the back burner until time and circumstances would give me the wherewithal to make it work.

So along comes retirement. Out to pasture. Geezerhood. Not me, I thought after a couple weeks, hanging around the old homestead, cleaning out the garage and other things my sweet bride had on her list. We're going to Alaska. And we're going to drive every long step of the way there and back. I want to see this country!

Thus started the planning. Now we all know that getting ready can be just about as much fun as the trip itself. I had a great time looking for information, and the trip ultimately became the destination.

All my life I've wanted an Airstream trailer. My Granddad had one that he hauled around on his many fishing trips to Florida. So early on, I was hooked. But if I were going to have an Airstream, I would also need just the right tow vehicle to make it work. The research started. What size Airstream, and what kind of vehicle? After tons of time looking at specs for vehicles and trailers, in the end I opted for the little Airstream Bambi and Toyota's new FJ Cruiser.

Next came the trip. What route to take? How much time should we budget to make the adventure fun and not just a marathon? What gear would we need? On and on the list grew.

Now I was indeed fortunate to marry up, and my bride (we celebrated our 42nd wedding anniversary on this trip in Alaska) is an amazingly good detail person. She would make lists of every potential need, and we would begin pulling the items together. I also realized that it would be great to talk to people who have actually made a similar trip. I quickly discovered that a good Rotarian friend of mine, George Atherholt, had full-timed in a 31-foot Airstream in Alaska for three years. What a resource! George gave me invaluable information.

It took Linda and me the better part of a year to bring all the plans together so we would be comfortable hitting the trail. At last on the morning of June 22, 2007, we pulled out of our driveway and pointed our little rig northwest toward Alaska. First stop, West Virginia.

Over the first few days, we developed a routine of driving and camping. We would drive between 250 and 300 miles a day, find a campground on or close to our route, explore the area and kick back for the evening. Next day, more of the same as we watched the miles roll by.

Linda kept a daily journal and here is an excerpt that typifies a day on the road:

Day 19, Tuesday, Left Fort Nelson at 7:20, 60 degrees, cloudy skies. Into the wilderness again. Steamboat Mountain, beautiful views. Stopped once for pictures. Best views aren't at pullouts, though. Saw a mother moose and calf. Managed a photo as we passed. Construction crews making repairs along the highway. Sign: Watch, fresh oil ahead.

After so many days of plains, we have arrived! These Rocky Mountains are beautiful. There are rocky rivers as well that I want to walk along and photograph from just the right angle. We've passed moose, caribou, sheep, goats and black bears alongside the road. The guy at the Rocky Mountain Lodge where we stopped for gas said the animals come down the mountains and lick the road surface for the minerals that wash down. He also said that yesterday a grizzly came to the area across the road from his station. Talked about the winters. He told us that it used to get down to 50 below zero but now only gets down to 20 below.

We had lunch at the Northern Rockies Lodge, hamburger and chicken sandwich served with fries plus water and iced tea, $36.40. Expensive but good.

The rivers (Toad, Trout, etc.) are so pretty. The palest, green turquoise. Fast water. Tom said it would be a good ride but would have to be warmer than today.

In places, the mountains are really majestic and purple or least a light shade of it. Just like the song says.

It rained off and on all day today, even snowed a tiny bit as we walked into the lodge for lunch.

Bumpy ride! Frost heaves everywhere making for slow going. Saw black bears again. Arrived at camp very tired.

We were amazed at how big this country is. From the rolling blue grass of Kentucky to the miles of cornfields in southern Illinois and Iowa, to the immense plains of South Dakota that stretched to the horizon and the amazing vistas of the mountains of Montana, we were constantly looking and pointing. I don't think either of us realized how truly big North America is until we pulled up to Canadian customs right outside of Shelby, Montana after 14 days on the road. We checked the map, computed our mileage and realized we were halfway to Alaska. We still had 2400 miles to go.

Canada proved to be challenging, not only because of the higher expense of just about everything we purchased, including gas sold by the liter that averaged about $4.50 to $5.00 a gallon, but the differences in lifestyle which were evident everywhere. Hey, they have a beautiful country and we adjusted pretty quickly. The Yukon Territory is as wild as Alaska, maybe having even more wilderness. Dawson Creek, British Columbia ushered us onto the Alaskan Highway, 1300 miles of road that will park you on the side if you don't give it the respect it deserves. Frost heaves that come from thawing and freezing right above the permafrost make for an interesting ride. For about three days between Whitehorse, Yukon Territory and Tok, Alaska we averaged 35 miles an hour.

Twenty-four days after leaving Southern Pines, we pulled into Fairbanks, Alaska. The little rig was as brown and grey as the gravel and mud it had ridden over. We were wiser, seasoned travelers, and we had driven the Alaska Highway.

We still looked forward to Denali, Anchorage, Palmer and the ride over the mountains on the Tok cut, then again the Alaska Highway and the long ride home. On Tuesday, August 22, 54 days and 11,034 miles later, the little rig pulled back into our driveway in Southern Pines. We had had one flat tire, and the windshield of the Cruiser suffered a couple of chips from rocks thrown up in road construction areas in the Yukon. Still, we can't wait to get back on the road. Rocking chairs on the porch? I don't think so. The kid who pitched his army blanket tent in his backyard 60 years ago is still alive and well. The only difference is his tent has morphed into a little Airstream Bambi.

The Perfect Stranger

The plan was to climb over the ridge from the little trout stream where I had been fishing all morning, pick up the Bronco, then drive up the mountain to our son Tommy's place for a quick lunch. After a short nap, I'd get back to the stream to fish the south fork until dark. Yep, that was the plan. Then I saw the boulder hanging out over the creek like a hammock. It was the perfect place to lie back and enjoy the scenery, which is just what I did. Listening to the sounds of the water rippling over the rocks soon put me to sleep, though, and when I awoke with a start, I thought, "Man, this is going to put a crimp in my afternoon plans. I'd better get a move on."

When I came out of the brush to the little gravel road where I had parked the Bronco, I was surprised to see an older man leaning up against the vehicle. I walked up slowly to the truck wondering all the while who he was and, more than that, what he wanted. The mountain community where our son lives is relatively unpopulated and has a private road serving the area. It's rare to see anyone on foot, especially someone of this individual's age.

"Whaddaya say, partner?" I said as I came up to the back of the Bronco, raised the window and put the tailgate down. "Something I can do for you?"

The old gentleman came around the corner of the truck and said, "You sure can, sir, if you have the time. I'm hoping you can give me a ride back to my cabin, which is just on the other side of the mountain. I started off fishing early this morning, and it seems as if I've sprained an ankle."

The old guy was dressed in the traditional mountain fly-fisherman's outfit: vest, khaki shirt, old moleskin trousers and hip boots of a style I hadn't seen in years. He limped rather severely, holding on to the Bronco all the while.

"Sit up on the tailgate," I said, "And I'll help you off with those hip boots.

He climbed up slowly, grimacing a little. "You wouldn't happen to have a cigarette?" he asked.

"No, sir. I quit smoking more than thirty years ago."

"Me too," he replied, "I quit a long time ago, but I made up my mind today that the next person I meet who has some cigarettes, I'm gonna bum one and try it again."

He was looking at me with an amused glint in his eyes as I gently grabbed the heel of his hurt ankle.

"I don't know, Bubba," I said. "This could hurt. Maybe I should run you down to the hospital and let them take a look at you."

"No, sir," he replied. "That's too much trouble. I've sprained this same ankle before. You know how once you hurt an ankle, it's always weak. I'll just wait till I get back to the cabin and we'll try to get it off there. It's an old boot and if need be, I'll just cut it off. No smokes, huh?"

"That's right," I replied. "No smokes."

There was something strange about the old guy that I couldn't quite put a finger on. He seemed out of place here on the side of the mountain, and yet he looked familiar.

"Have I met you somewhere before?"

"I don't think so," he replied. "I haven't been down in this hollow in several years. You know, about those cigarettes, isn't it funny how the things we enjoy the most are either not good for you or illegal. I smoked a bunch and enjoyed it a bunch but quit because I was smart enough to know that they could kill me. And drinking, now I enjoy a slight touch of fine scotch as much as the next guy. And even if the doctor says it's not good for me, I'm still gonna have a toddy in the evening."

The old timer was on a roll, and he was also cutting into my plan for the afternoon.

"Well, I tell you what, old sport. Let me help you get in the Bronco. We'll go on back to your place and I'll help you get settled. Is anyone there to give you a hand? I wish you would let me take you to the emergency room."

"I'll be fine," he said. "When we get to the house, I'll get us some lunch if you have the time. I've got a few trout I'll fry up, and I'll make us a great salad with fixings I got down at the farmers market. How did you do this morning?"

I had broken down the gentleman's fly rod, an old bamboo one, and put it along with his creel in the back. While doing it, I noticed that his equipment was well worn but expensive.

"Oh, I caught several six- and seven-inchers. Nothing I would want to keep."

I cranked the Bronco and eased up the mountain trail.

"You're gonna have to show me the way."

"It's not too far. Just keep on this road till it forks at the top of the mountain, then down to the little wooden bridge, ford Call Creek, and it's just a short piece from there. He noticed the expression on my face when he said ford. "Don't worry, the creek there is only six or eight inches deep. By the way, my name is Sam Call. I own most of this mountain. Been in the family for years."

On the ride to his cabin, we talked about trout fishing, hunting, the mild winter we just had, and anything two perfect strangers would converse about.

"There's the fork, about a mile to the little bridge and then across the creek and home. I can't tell you how much I appreciate this."

"Glad to help out," I said. "You live in a pretty area."

"Yeah, it's about time for the laurel to bloom. It really will be beautiful then. Kinda quiet up here. I like that."

We got to the little wooden bridge over the creek.

"I had to build the bridge. The creek's too deep to cross here. The ford is right up ahead."

The small gravel road, more like a path, was overhung with low limbs from the brush on both sides. It was like entering a tunnel. When we came up over the rise, there sat his cabin, nestled on a low ridge. The scene was as picturesque as any postcard. His house was a two-story structure with a porch that wrapped around the entire building. The ground floor was made of logs, and the second level was covered with bark siding. The entire setting was unbelievably striking, and I expressed that to the old fellow.

"I've enjoyed it here. As a matter of fact, I haven't been off the mountain much, just for supplies and materials when I was building the cabin. Come on in. I want to give you something for helping me out today."

"You don't have to do that," I said as I unloaded his fishing gear out of the Bronco and helped him up the stairs to the front porch.

"Let's try and get those boots off."

He sat down on a rocker right by the front door and I gently pulled the boot expecting a yelp at any minute. It slipped right off.

"Well, how about that," he said. "Seems as if the ankle has gone down some."

I helped him off with the other boot.

"Well, old sport, I appreciate the lunch offer but I'm gonna try to get in a little more fishing this afternoon. So I'm back over the mountain."

"Wait just a second," he said, "Come on in. I've got something for you that'll help in your trout fishing."

I went in the cabin with the old gentleman and he hobbled up the stairs. I was awe struck by the stone fireplace that stretched across one wall of the main room.

"It took me a year to build that fireplace," he said as he came back down the stairs leaning heavily on the banister.

"It's beautiful. I've never seen anything like it."

"I hauled the rocks in a horse-drawn wagon from the creek we crossed. It was a labor of love. Here, I know you're in a hurry. I want you to have this."

The old guy deposited a fishing fly in my hand.

"I tie them myself and I use feathers from wood ducks. That style is one of my favorites. It'll catch you a trout. Now you come back when you have more time, and I'll show you some photos of nice catches I've made in Call Creek. Tonight, to celebrate finding a new friend, I'm breaking out my Cuban cigars and I'll have one with a touch of single malt before bed."

I thanked him and said good-bye, climbed into the Bronco, stuck the fishing fly up over the sun visor on the passenger side and hustled on back to Tom's place to grab a bite. After my late lunch, I found the afternoon was too far gone to do any serious fishing, so I decided to wait until Tom got home from work, then we would ride over to Blowing Rock for supper.

That evening during a great dinner at Canyons Restaurant, I told him about my morning experience and the old guy I had met.

Tommy looked funny at me and then laughed and said, "You're pulling my leg, Dad. You must have been dreaming longer than you thought down at the creek. When we get home, I'll show you an old magazine from 1965 featuring Sam Call and how he died in a cabin fire. They seem to think he fell asleep smoking. The only thing left from the blaze was the giant stone chimney. I think it's still there."

Needless to say, the rest of the evening was spent in pondering what I thought had happened. The only answer was that I'd dreamed the whole episode while napping by the creek. Maybe, we finally decided, I had read the story in a magazine on an earlier visit to Tom's house and forgot about it, thus creating fodder for the dream.

The next morning, still thinking about the previous day's events, I headed home to catch up on some overdue chores. The sun was blazing out of the east, and I reached over to the passenger side sun visor and lowered it.

A hand-tied fishing fly, unmistakably made from wood duck feathers, fell on the seat.

The Great Unloading

I was really quite proud of myself. Here it was going on seven months in the New Year of 2015 and I had kept almost all my New Year's resolutions. Nope, what was it George Washington said? "I cannot tell a lie." I didn't keep three and honestly can't even remember what they were. The fourth one I'm bound to keep because the lady of the house is now well and kicking after major back surgery, and hot after me to clean out my garage. That New Year's resolution must have been made under duress because I do recall writing it down somewhere, and I don't usually write those things down.

"I expect the 'pickers' from the history channel to show up here some morning and ask permission to scrounge through your garage to see if they can find anything worthwhile. I'm sure they could find a lot of stuff; worthwhile might be iffy." Linda, my bride, seems to have acquired a little more sarcasm since her recent bout at the hospital. She's feeling a lot better with no back pain. I think I'll be cleaning out the garage tomorrow.

The first chore of what would be known as the Great Unloading was to move all the big stuff out into the driveway. The old Bronco came first. Our son Tommy's Mustang had to stay because when he was here on a recent visit, he removed the battery and radiator and propped them in a corner. He promised to take care of them on his next sojourn to Southern Pines. I had talked to him the evening before and told him, "Son, you need to get down here and pick up your stuff and take it back to your mountain. You've also got to get this Mustang."

Tommy's '89 Mustang is a classic. It was his college car and has been stored in my garage since we located to Moore County. He's a building contractor living on a mountaintop close to Fleetwood in the Boone area.

"Dad, I've got nowhere to put it until I finish building my storage/garage building. Don't throw any of my things away. I'll come down in a couple of weeks."

I decided to just put his stuff in a pile in the corner. After I got the bicycles and all the paraphernalia that went with them in the drive, I tackled my fishing equipment. Rods and reels, spinning outfits, lures in boxes and bait cans and rod holders, paddles and life jackets and boat cushions, and I found one bait casting reel I thought I had lost years ago. Also under a table were two skeet throwers— one a manual stick thrower, the other a spring-loaded job. I had no idea where they came from. Had to be Tommy's, I thought.

Under the workbench I spotted an old metal footlocker I had in college. It was dust-covered and grungy. I wiped it off with a wet rag then hauled it outside. I pulled up a dove stool, opened the ancient box and saw it was filled with some of my Boy Scout equipment from years ago. I was just getting ready to go through the old discoveries when Linda came out the back door and said she was on the way to church for a meeting.

"I'm proud of you, honey," she said. "Now, don't get sidetracked looking through all that stuff. I'll be back in a little while and help you."

"Okay, Babe," I replied as I dug into the locker. The first thing I pulled out was my official Boy Scout cook kit, which was a little black and sooty. It was still in its cloth sheath, ready to go. I put it aside to clean up later. Next was a compass with a missing lens (still worked though), a camping knife, fork and spoon in a molded leather holder, a broken utility knife with half a blade, an aluminum canteen, and a hatchet with a cracked handle. Good stuff, I thought. This equipment was prime in its day. Belk in downtown Aberdeen used to be the dealer for official Boy Scout equipment. They sold everything from uniforms to cooking gear. When I was in town, I always made a tour of Belk and the counter where the newest gear was displayed.

Rarely did I, or any of my friends, have the money to buy the latest Boy Scout registered equipment; and if one of us did happen to get something from the wish counter, he was envied by the entire troop.

Portions of my uniform were in the locker: a green cloth web belt for a 28-inch waist, khaki shorts, a Scout kerchief, and my merit badge sash with all the badges I had earned while active in old Troop 206.

I obtained the rank of Life while in the Boy Scouts, and one of my biggest regrets was not becoming an Eagle. I was almost there with all the qualifications but along came the age of 16, and with it a driver's license, sports and girls. The rank of Eagle was put on the back shelf until it was too late.

In the very bottom of the locker was my Order of the Arrow (OA) sash. It brought back tons of memories. Back when our troop was very active, we were part of the charter members of OA.

I took my ordeal and was tapped as a member at Camp Durant near Raleigh. Part of the ordeal was to overnight in the woods alone with just a bedroll, then go through a day of silence with only a bologna sandwich for lunch. Afterwards, we did odd jobs at the camp.

That evening, around a blazing bonfire, we were tapped on the shoulder by an official in full Indian regalia and became members of the Order of the Arrow, a big event for a youngster of fourteen.

The old sash was yellowed with age but still valuable to me, so I put it aside along with the merit badges for safekeeping. In the distance, I could hear thunder booming, and it looked as if the predicted rain was on the way. I dragged all the stuff back into the garage with the exception of the skeet throwers, which I put in the back of the Bronco.

Tomorrow, I'll finish this. No, I can't tomorrow. Supposed to go fishing. Maybe I can finish it next week. No, we're supposed to go to the beach next week. Makes no difference. I've got the rest of the summer to get all this squared away, and at least now I know where some of my good stuff is.

I went inside with my two scout sashes as the rain rolled in over the pines. Now I need to find a safe place to put these, I thought. Maybe Linda can help me when she gets home. She's gonna love seeing these old scout badges, but I've got to convince her that the rest of the garage stuff is not migrating to the house.

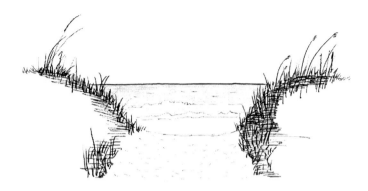

The Beach Boys

After the summer solstice and later when August comes on blazing and the dogs start digging holes in the shrubbery beds looking for some cool, there is only one thing for me that will cure what is known as the dog days of summer, and that's a camping trip to the beach.

Now admittedly, my camping has evolved over the years from pup tents to bigger tents to motel rooms. The motel rooms came after marriage when my bride jokingly declared that the Holiday Inn would be roughing it enough. Finally, we found the best of all worlds, a small self-contained 19-foot Airstream trailer with all the benefits of home that you can take to the woods.

We've had the little Stream, as we call her, for about three years and she has added so much to our travels around this great country. After the initial purchase and a couple of small trial runs, we ventured off on our first mega trip, driving to Alaska and back via the Alaska Highway. This adventure, which took two months, made our current plans of a late summer beach outing seem rather miniscule.

It takes a day or two to get the Stream loaded and ready to roll; but once you do and are on the road, a whole different world stretches to the horizon. Probably the biggest advantage of traveling with your house hitched to your SUV is meeting new people along the way. Without fail, we have met some of the finest and also some of the strangest on the trail. This late summer trip would prove no different. Huntington Beach is a South Carolina state park located just below Murrells Inlet. Three miles of pristine untouched beach strand makes this one of the South's most desired camping parks and our destination for this late summer outing. It's only about three hours from Southern Pines, so by five o'clock that afternoon we were on our site, set up and ready to enjoy. School had already started in South Carolina, and the park wasn't crowded at all.

Linda was in the Stream preparing a light supper, so I decided to stroll to the beach and pick out a couple of fishing spots for later in the week. The walk to the strand is a thing of beauty itself. The park people have cut a walkway through the old myrtle bushes and live oaks that line the trail. When you enter the cool shade of those trees, you're transported back in time 200 years. After about a quarter mile, I stepped out of the coolness into blazing bright sunlight reflecting off white powder sand and clear blue ocean. It was all I could do just to take it all in. I meandered on out to stick my toes in the Atlantic, then turned and walked up the beach. Huge puffy cumulus clouds banked up just inland like stacks of giant cotton balls. I stopped to absorb all the beauty of the beach at its best.

On the way back to the campsite, I met a young fellow accompanying an older gentleman who appeared to be his grandfather. They were just beginning the walk through the myrtles to the ocean. The old guy was bent over with age and seemed to be struggling with the effort required to plow through the sand.

"It's a pretty good hike out to the beach," I said, more for the younger guy.

I knew that the old fellow was going to have his hands full making the hard trek in that heat.

"We know. He wants to make it on his own," he replied.

"Well, good luck and be careful." I turned toward our campsite hoping they would be all right.

Back at the Airstream, I checked with Linda and told her about meeting the couple trudging to the beach.

"Why don't you go back and check on them? It's a while until supper. When I finish up here, I'll come out and join you and we'll hang out on the beach. I just have to put this salad together."

"Okay," I replied. "I'll take the chairs. Probably they're there by now. See you in a little bit."

I grabbed the beach chairs and retraced my steps.

They were just to the end of the myrtle bushes where the walk really became grueling.

"Y'all are doing okay," I said as I came up to them.

The younger guy was standing close to his old partner, helping him hold on to the railing of the walkway that traversed the last wet area. After that, there was nothing but hard walking in soft sand through the dunes to the beach. A tough hike for anybody, but almost impossible, I thought, for this fellow.

"You know, I have these beach chairs," I said to the older guy. "What if you sit down in one of these and your friend and I just tote you the rest of the way?"

"Nah," he said as he squinted up at me from his bent over position.

"You might have to carry me back, though," he said, wheezing out a dry laugh.

"Okay, sport," I replied. "The Marine Corps taught me how to carry around a lot of things, including people. You just holler if you need help."

I looked over at the young guy.

"I'll be just down the beach a ways if you need me."

Linda showed up a little later. I had the chairs ready and she had brought snacks and the books we were reading.

"I met the people you were talking about on my way out. They are just about here."

I looked down the beach and saw the determined couple emerge from the dunes. The younger guy put up a beach umbrella and a couple chairs, and both of them sat down. They looked exhausted.

The old gentleman's odyssey wasn't over yet, though. A few minutes later, I noticed both of them get up from their chairs and slowly head to the water. The tide was all the way out.

They reached water's edge, and the old guy stood there looking toward the distant horizon where thunderheads were building. Every now and then, heat lightning would flash through the tops of the tall clouds. I told Linda, "Hon, I'm gonna walk down there and talk to these folks. I'll be back in a few minutes."

The young guy saw me walking toward them and came over to meet me. The old fellow continued to stare out over the ocean.

"Thanks for your offer to help back there," he said, glancing toward the dunes. "Dad just wanted to do it himself."

"That's amazing. I thought he was your grandfather. How old is he?"

"He'll be 97 in October. We've been coming to this beach every summer since I was a baby. It's one of his favorite places. My wife and kids are back at our campsite. He couldn't wait to get to the ocean, so I brought him on down. He has slowed down a lot this year.

"I tell you, he's a determined gentleman," I replied. "What did he do in his working life?"

"He was a forester and managed timber farms for several big plantations in South Carolina. That was before the paper companies bought up all the timberland."

Small world, I thought. I bet he knew my grandfather who was also a timber farmer.

"Well, sport, we're heading back for supper. You sure I can't help get him back?"

"No, he's going to lie down and rest a bit, and then we'll make the trek."

When Linda and I walked back to the cut through the dunes, I noticed that the old guy had lain down under the umbrella with a hat pulled over his eyes, and his son was at the water's edge almost standing in his dad's footsteps, looking toward the horizon. Thunderheads continued to flash summer lightning across the lowering, late afternoon sky.

The "Soule" of a Good Hunt

Good night nurse, it was hot! If you're in the Sandhills in the summer, you know it's gonna be warm; but the spell we were having was one of those scorching, fry-an-egg-on-the-sidewalk, smoking, summer days that had the dogs digging in the shrubbery looking for some cool.

I was out in my garage where I keep a lot of hunting and fishing paraphernalia, determined to put it in some semblance of order. The old saying that empty space will fill itself is doubly true in my case. There were duck decoys all over my workbench. I had left them there at the close of hunting season in January with the idea that if I left out the ones that needed repainting, I would get to it before the next season rolled around. Like a lot of good intentions, this one was not realized. I backed the old Bronco out in the driveway to give me some working room and set up a portable table, seeing as how my workbench was loaded down. Before I could get to work, though, I plugged in a couple fans. It didn't help a lot, but the moving air made my workspace bearable.

Linda, my bride of 40 something years was in France with an old friend taking watercolor painting classes at a historic chateau south of Normandy. I had been on my own for a little over a week, and this garage clean-up was high on the list for me to do before she came home.

I could hear thunder rumbling down close to Aberdeen. Hopefully, I thought, we'd get some rain.

My decoy paint was not useable, having dried as hard as a dirt clod; so I began to put my old Bean decoys that needed painting on a shelf out of the way to take care of later.

I really need to re-rig my green head decoys with weights anyway. A lot of 'em lost theirs in the final days of hunting last year. But, I thought, that can wait too; this old goose decoy has got to have some help.

Sometime during the winter my elk horn mount, a gift from a good neighbor, had fallen and broken the head slap off the decoy, and it was one of my favorites. That's what I get for leaving it on the workbench.

A Bean decoy by George Soule is a work of art, and the ones I had acquired in my early days of duck hunting had increased in value. I still insist on hunting over them, though.

What's a working decoy for? Not to sit on a shelf and gather dust, or get busted by an errant elk horn.

Thunder was becoming more evident now, and I could smell rain in the air. I dragged a chair closer to the open garage door and turned the fan more in my direction.

I had found a tube of glue in one of my cabinets. On its side was written Miracle glue. Can glue anything. I put a dab on the goose decoy neck and another dab on the body and holding them together, I grabbed a cold beer from my little garage refrigerator and kicked back in the camp chair. Who says I can't multi-task.

My garage door faces west, and I could see tall, cumulous clouds building gray and dark and moving in my direction. Every now and then, a thunderclap would rock the windows and I would count to six to see how far away the storm was.

Somewhere in my brain's bank of useless information, I remembered that every six seconds counted after a thunder rumble equates to a mile that the storm is from your location. A cool breeze blew in from the driveway, and I propped the goose up next to the door to help the glue dry and thought back to the last time I used the decoy.

Many, many years ago, when Paddle, my yellow lab, was in her prime, Tom Bobo and Bob Rudolph, my good hunting buddies, and I were duck hunting the brand new Falls of the Neuse Lake. This lake was built to provide flood control for the folks downstream on the Neuse River. This wasn't a first hunt on the lake for us; you might say we were charter members, having hunted the lake in canoes while the Neuse slowly spread out above the dam, providing great habitat for migrating waterfowl and super hunting for enterprising duck hunters.

On this trip, however, we were on a new tack. The lake was partially full, and we had heard that Canada Geese were using the area on their migration south. In those days before Canadas figured out that they really didn't have to migrate, that they could come down here and stay, sort of like some of our favorite Yankee friends, a Canada goose this far west was unheard of.

So that frosty, cold, overcast morning found us hunkered down in a makeshift blind on a small island on the northwest side of the lake. The morning had been uneventful thus far and like most duck hunters, we were determined to give the day enough time. If nothing else, a duck hunter is ever the optimist. It never fails.

As I was pouring a cup of hot coffee from my thermos and just before I offered Tom a cup, Bob motioned for me to be quiet. I also noticed Paddle was on full alert, and I knew something was up, but I couldn't see a thing in the sky. Then I heard them. A group of five Canadas came around the northern tree line and were zeroed in on the pair of goose decoys we had placed on the outside of our duck spread. They came in high, circled around out of range a time or two and sat down about a hundred yards from the decoys.

From then on, it was a waiting game. They would swim up almost in range then drift back, swim up, drift back. This went on for about thirty minutes or so before they finally committed, and then we lowered the boom on them.

In those days, the limit for migratory geese was one per hunter, and we had three on the water. Paddle was long gone on the farthest retrieve after the goose I had winged, and I knew it wouldn't be easy.

She finally caught the bird after a hard swim of more than a hundred yards and turned back into the wind toward the island. She was making absolutely no headway, and Bob and I jumped into the boat to help her.

I was in the stern running the kicker and Bob was in the bow. When we reached Paddle, she was hanging on for dear life. Her grip on the goose was actually keeping her from going under. Bob grabbed the bird and I grabbed Paddle, hoisted her into the boat and headed back to the island to pick up the other two geese.

Thunder was booming more ominously now, and I moved farther back into the garage, enjoying the breath of cool air. I carried the old goose decoy with me and held it in my lap while I watched the storm approach. The memory of that hunt on the Falls of the Neuse brought the decoy into better perspective. It was beat up and scratched, a lot of the paint was peeled off, and I could see where some shot from a stray duck load had hit it a time or two. But Paddle and I had watched beautiful sunrises over this Soule piece of art; and if the good Lord lets me, I hope to see a few more. It looks as if my miracle glue is holding.

Black Duck Paradise

A brisk wind was blowing out of the northeast. It had a little bite to it and felt good after the unseasonably warm weather we had been experiencing. Paddle, my yellow Lab, and I were in the backyard loading up the boat. As a matter of fact, Paddle was already in the boat, ready to go. She would look at me whimpering with excitement, wanting to do what she was bred for, duck hunting.

For me it was the best of all worlds. Tomorrow, duck season would come back in after the early teasers in October and November. Those few short days were just enough to get hunters wired with anticipation for the real season in December. And if that excitement weren't enough, it was only six days until Christmas.

It's a wonder I wasn't in the boat whining with Paddle. We had a good plan. Early in the morning around four o'clock, I was to ride up to Hyco Lake, boat in tow, launch at the landing on the north end, duck hunt at our special spot until noon, then motor down to Bubba's cabin and wait for him to show up toward evening. Bubba's cabin is located on a creek tributary and sits high on a ridge overlooking the lake. The view in winter with all the leaves off the trees is spectacular. Beginning at the cabin and meandering down the ridge are steps leading to a boathouse and dock where I would moor my little duck boat for the duration of the hunt. Bubba has a big johnboat that we planned to use for the rest of the weekend.

It was rare that Bubba missed an opening day, but his textile mill needed him and try as he might, he couldn't get away from an important conference call. I would miss his company, but sometimes I enjoy the wild all by myself, and as long as Paddle is along, I rarely get lonesome.

My boat is a little Armstrong Widgeon model. She's only twelve feet long with a four-foot beam, almost like a layout rig and extremely stable, impossible to turn over. She's rated for a ten-horse kicker, which will get her up on plane quickly and zip across the water like a little speedboat. With decoys, hunting gear and dog, the little boat is comfortable, and I've spent a lot of time in her, pursuing the noble waterfowl. I had already hooked her to the Bronco and was making sure that the fuel tank was full when Linda, my bride, came to the back door with the message that Bubba wanted me to call him back as soon as I could. Wonder what's going on with that boy, I thought.

The decoy spread I planned called for six mallards—hens and drakes, three black ducks, and a couple of Canada Geese thrown in for good measure. I was using my LL Bean cork decoys, although they weigh a lot more than the molded plastic models I use when I'm shooting impoundments. On the water, the Bean decoys look more like real ducks. I picked out the ones that I had just had repainted by the Decoy Factory in Maryland. They looked great, and if any ducks were flying in the morning, I was sure they would pay us a visit.

It didn't take long to finish loading the rest of the hunting paraphernalia, then I went inside to give Bubba a call. Paddle refused to leave the boat and would probably stay there until we left in the early morning, if I let her. That little dog was excited.

"Hey, Bubba, what's up? I've got the boat all loaded, and I'll be trucking outta here at four a.m. You sure you can't go?"

"Man, I wish. But duty calls. It also looks as if I can't get there until late. You know where the cabin key is. Let yourself in and I'll be there as soon as I can. Steaks and all the fixings are in the fridge. Why don't you go ahead and grill 'em and I hope to be there in time to help eat 'em. Remember, I like mine rare," he said, laughing.

"I think this is nothing but a ploy to get me to do all the work," I replied. "If I'm real hungry, I might eat your steak as well as mine."

After a little more conversation about supplies and timing, we rang off and I resumed my efforts getting ready. I slept in the guest room that night, so as not to wake Linda when the alarm clock woke me. By four-thirty, Paddle was in her favorite spot, sitting in the passenger's seat, and we were on our way to the lake and another great adventure. A half moon was breaking through a low overcast, providing enough light to help in launching the boat, and in record time, I had the little Widgeon tied to the landing dock. I parked the Bronco and trailer next to a fence bordering the gravel lot and was surprised to see that mine was the only vehicle there. I thought for sure there would be more hunters, especially since it was opening day of the late season. The motor fired on the first pull, and I eased away from the landing area, made the turn south and poured on the juice. Running at night in a little boat has a thrill all its own, but it also has dangers that accompany the experience. Constant vigilance to avoid floating debris and other boats had me on the lookout for anything unusual on the horizon.

Hyco Lake is a deep-water lake and was built in the early sixties by Carolina Power and Light Company (now Duke Energy Progress) as a cooling reservoir for their generating plant. Migrating waterfowl use the lake to rest on their way south and are quite prevalent during cold snaps up north. I was hoping the recent snowfall around Maryland would hurry a few my way. Last duck season, Bubba and I discovered a thirty-foot-wide water ditch that runs about a mile to the power plant. The canal is used to supply cooling water for their generators. It was cabled across to keep out big boats, but our little crafts had no problem getting under. On the east side of the ditch is an opening that leads to a sheltered area of water, almost like a small lake. This is our honey hole, the spot we would later name Black Duck Paradise. The run to the ditch took about forty minutes, and a grey tint was in the eastern sky as I hurriedly put out the decoys: mallards in a bunch and geese and black ducks off to the side. I pulled the boat into a small slough, and Paddle and I hunkered down under alders that grew on the bank right to the water. We made it just in time to legally shoot and had just gotten settled with shotgun loaded when whistling wings could be heard right over us. I didn't dare look up but watched Paddle as her head moved with the flight of the ducks. I could tell that they were circling, so I blew a soft chuckling welcome on my duck call. That did it.

They came in low, right in front, wings locked, big yellow legs down like landing gear. It was a classic. Three shots and three big mallards for Christmas dinner. I sent Paddle to retrieve, and she was in the water like an otter. I stood up grinning. It was going to be a great season.

Where Eagles Soar

The granddaddy of all mule deer was resting in his favorite spot high on the ridge overlooking the valley below. He had discovered this hideaway years before during a blinding snowstorm, and it had since become the spot to survey his entire kingdom. A little outcrop impossible to be seen from lower elevations, it served as a good place to while away the day until evening and time to head to the valley for food. A gravel dirt road runs north to south of the small valley, and he watched as a little red truck followed by a bigger four-wheel drive vehicle stirred up the dust way down below. He paid little attention to the commotion as an eagle soared high above. The red truck pulled up the rocky drive to the two-room cabin and skidded to a stop. The Ford Bronco was right behind him. A big burley guy, almost too big for the vehicle, oozed out the driver's side and reached back in to grab a pouch of Red Man chewing tobacco off the dash. He watched as four men piled out of the Bronco. "Well, guys, this is it. Ain't much to look at, but she'll keep you warm and dry if you treat her right. How 'bout a chew?" They all turned him down, but one of the four opened the back of the Bronco and reached into a cooler.

"I can use this beer. It's been a long day since North Carolina. How about it, Red? You join us?"

"Naw, I've got to head back in just a bit. My sister is cooking up her famous stew tonight, and I need to get there in time for supper or my worthless brother-in-law will eat it all. Let me show you about the place."

The tiny mountain cabin was to be their home for the next ten days as they pursued the wily mule deer. Red unhooked a big latch at the top of the door and an identical one at the bottom and screeched the door open. "I'll spray that with W-D before I leave."

They walked in and crowded around the little room. The four were silent as Red started to explain the peculiarities of the cabin.

"The sleeping area is upstairs. There are six bunks, and all you'll need is your sleeping bags. And you'll need those 'cause it gets cold up here at night. The fireplace will keep you warm and toasty though, especially when you fire up Waltzing Matilda. He pointed to a monster black wood cookstove. I'll tell you about her in a minute. The milk cans are to haul water in. See that cistern over the sink? Siphon water out of a can into the cistern, open this valve right here, and as they say in France, 'Voila,' all the comforts of home. Now, let's get the lay of the land."

They all followed Red back outside and formed a half circle as he continued to hold forth.

"On the side of the cabin is the wood shed. Now last time I checked, there was a family of skunks living in there. I haven't seen one yet. You can smell 'em, though. They won't bother you. Just make a little noise before you open the door. Nothing worse than a surprised skunk. Up the road is where you'll find the water. A spring, or almost an artesian well. Clear, cold, fresh mountain water. You'll love it. Fill those milk cans about half full; they're heavy and can tip over. That would make for a mess in your new rental Bronco."

"Now, let's check out the hunting area. See that valley there?" Red pointed across to the ridge on the other side.

"Pretty, ain't it? Well, you can't hunt there. It's posted. Owned by, believe it or not, a bunch of trout fishermen. Let's walk out here."

The crew dutifully followed Red out to the center of the road.

"Those mountains to the south and to the north are where the deer are anyway. They come down off the ridges at night to feed and go back up before day to rest. A simple hunt. You just got to get 'em coming or going. Red chuckled at his little witticism. The other four just looked at each other.

Wayne, the one who had put the hunt together, said, "Man, those mountains are straight up. How are we supposed to get up there?"

"Very carefully," Red chuckled again. He was enjoying his stint as instructor. "Naw, man, it ain't hard. Do like the deer do. They don't tackle those ridges head on; they go from side to side. You'll know when you get up there and see their trails. You'll figure it out. Oh, one more thing. Come on back inside."

They all trooped dutifully behind him.

"On the counter over the sink is a weather radio. I brought extra batteries. Listen to it everyday. If it says that a front is roaring in here from the northwest, saddle up that Bronco and head to the lowlands. This place gets from 300 to 500 inches of snow a season. The only thing that can get in here after a storm are snowmobiles driven by experienced rangers. I'd hate for you to have to winter up here."

After spraying the door and explaining about the stove, Red said,"Okay, boys, I've got to go. One more warning."

The good old boy façade fell from Red as if he had just taken off a coat.

"Wayne has assured me that you all know what you're doing in the woods, and I took him at his word. These Wasatch Mountains can kill you. The authorities are still looking for a hunter that disappeared a couple of years back. He was hunting out of a cabin just on the other side of the water hole. There's a bunch of little creatures on these mountains that can scatter your bones about, so whatever you do, be careful."

The group went back outside and Red said. "One for the road." He stuffed a big wad of Red Man in his jaw, crammed himself into his little red truck, and rattled off.

They watched as the pick-up rambled down the road. DATSUN was emblazed across the tailgate.

"I didn't think they still made Datsuns." Tom, the tallest of the hunters, said.

"They just changed their name. I believe they're now Nissan."

"Okay, I'm a little smarter. One thing's for sure, though. If Red gains any more weight, he's gonna need a shoehorn to get in it. Let's unload this stuff."

The four grabbed gear from the back of the truck and shortly had most of it inside. Tom reached way in and pulled out his encased rifle. He looked up the road where the dust was just settling from Red's truck. An eagle soared high in the softening twilight.

"Well, tomorrow it begins," he thought.

The mule deer was already heading down from his lofty perch to feed.

Dance with the Mule Deer

Night was rapidly falling as the four men gathered around the fireplace looking for a little warmth.

"Red was right, boys. It sure does get cold when the sun goes down. I'm gonna get some more firewood to hold us for a while. We're also going to need water. How about a couple of you reprobates making a water run while I keep the fire going."

"Come on, Blake," Tom said as Bubba walked out the door heading to the wood shed. "Let Bubba do battle with the skunks. We'll find the water."

He hoisted a milk can that was to be one of their water containers and trudged toward the truck. Blake also grabbed a can and followed.

"I'll have the wood stove going and be ready for the water when y'all get back," said Wayne, the declared chief cook of the hunting trip, as he stuffed paper and kindling in the black monster of a wood stove.

"Watch out for the skunks!" Tom jovially warned Bubba as they drove off to look for the water hole. Red, the owner of the little place, had warned the four men about the skunks living in the wood shed during his introduction to the cabin and the surrounding mountains the four would be hunting for the next ten days.

Wayne had put the trip together weeks before, and when asked, the other three had enthusiastically agreed to join him. They were in the Wasatch Mountain Range of Utah, mule deer hunting. The cabin that was to be their hunting base belonged to an acquaintance Wayne had met. The cabin was rustic to say the least, with no electricity or running water. It provided the basic necessities, and that was it. The four men were experts in the outdoors, though, and the sparseness of their surroundings gave them a chance to test their talents.

Bubba came back in the cabin with an armload of wood as Wayne lit up the cook stove. "Red was right. There is definitely skunk smell around the wood shed, but I believe they have moved. At least I didn't have an encounter." Wood smoke was rolling out the stove and rapidly filling the room. "Hey, Wayne what's wrong with that thing?" Bubba asked as he headed for the door, coughing.

"I don't know, the chimney's not drafting." He followed Bubba out the door, tears streaming from his eyes. Maybe it'll do better when the flue warms up."

About that time Tom and Blake drove up from their water run.

"Wayne, you didn't set the place on fire already? We've got to have some place to sleep this evening." Blake laughed.

"Nah, I'm trying to get that dumb stove to work, that's all."

After a bit, the cabin began to clear out and the men could see smoke coming out the chimney. Wayne went back inside and started to prepare supper. The old wood stove rapidly heated the cabin, and the men began going through their gear getting ready for the next day. After a great dinner of almost homemade stew, Wayne pulled a topographic map from his pack and the four sorted out where each one would hunt the next day.

"I'm going out in the morning before dawn," Blake said after he looked over his hunting area.

"I'll join you since I'll be on the ridge next to yours." Wayne replied. "How about you other boys?"

"I'm gonna wait," Tom said. "I'm not gonna try and climb that mountain in the dark, especially since I don't know where I'm going. You boys are crazy. How about you, Bubba?"

"I'm with you, Tom. I figure we have ten days to figure this out, and I plan to go home in one piece. Remember how dangerous this place is, according to Red. Tomorrow is going to be a reconnoitering day for me. If I see a deer, he's outta luck. If I don't, that's all right, too."

The four sat around the fire enjoying themselves with conversations about past hunts.

"Well, I'm hitting the hay. It's been a long day, and I'm in for an early morning," said Blake. "Y'all know where the outhouse is. Don't wake me during your evening constitutionals."

"Yeah, right," Bubba chuckled. "At 14 degrees, the first will surely be the fastest."

They all laughed, and Wayne and Bubba followed Blake up to the cabin's bunk room.

"I'll be right with you jokers," Tom said. "I want to see what the moon's doing."

He walked out on the small front porch. The sky was a deep black punched through with a million stars, a sight you can only see in the wilderness. As he gazed at the ridge line across the valley, a meteor blazed across the blackness. A good luck sign, he thought and went in to bed.

Blake and Wayne were gone when Tom and Bubba got up the next morning, so they had a quick snack for breakfast and grabbed the packs they had filled the evening before. In no time, they were on the gravel road that led up the valley to the ridges they were going to hunt. Dawn was just a hint of grey when they separated.

"Well, I'll see you this evening, a little after dark, I reckon. You be careful," Tom told Bubba as he began to head toward the ridge looming before him.

"Yeah, you too." Bubba said. When Tom looked back, Bubba had faded away into the predawn grayness almost as if he hadn't been there at all.

The climb was grueling. A combination of altitude and unfamiliarity with the surroundings made for slow going, and noon found Tom less than half way up the mountain. Time to stop, he thought, breathing hard. At this rate, if I'm not careful I could become a statistic like the fellow down the road. He was thinking about a man who had been hunting the area a couple of years before and had disappeared. Tom sat down on fallen birch tree and ate his lunch. The sun had yet to appear over the ridge. After a bit, he said to himself, "I'll make one more push and settle in for the day."

Another climb, moving left to right, following deer trails found him at the edge of a small flat broom straw area of about three acres. This is the spot, he thought and settled down, his back to an aspen with broom straw all around. What a great place. A bright sun came over the ridge warming him; and he laid back, head on his pack, and took a nap.

Close to dark, Tom began his trek back down toward the cabin. Further up, on top of the ridge, a giant mule deer stretched from his day's sleep and also headed down the mountain.

The four men settled into a routine and the days flew by. No one was successful in taking a deer, but Wayne came close late one evening, missing his shot as the deer sensed the hunter and dove into a heavily brushed cut that went over the ridge. That evening, they sat around the supper table, tired after another day on the mountain.

"Well, boys, only three more days. Somebody's got to get lucky," Blake said. "I'm afraid the weather is getting ready to change. Remember what Red said about hightailing out of here if the weather radio said a northwest storm was brewing, and yesterday they said one is on the way. Tomorrow could be our last day."

"Well, they can't say we didn't try," Bubba said. "I'm tired. I'll see y'all in the morning."

The other three talked about their plans for what could be the final day as Bubba went up to bed.

"I've got a great spot on my ridge and I'm gonna give it one more shot tomorrow," Tom said. "After that, I think we all ought to consider getting ready to move out. We sure don't want to get snowed in up here."

The next morning, Tom, usually the last to leave the hut, was the first. Well, what do you know? Looks as if the rest of the boys are sleeping in, he thought. Not really a bad idea. But since I'm this far, I might as well go on up to my pasture. He had claimed ownership of the little flat broom straw field and was looking forward to spending the last hunt day there. The trail was a lot easier now, and he was more acclimated to the altitude, so just before noon, he was in his favorite spot ready to eat lunch. A bright sun peeked over the ridge highlighting strips of clouds. They look like mares tails, he thought. That could be a real harbinger of bad weather on the way. We really do need to head out in the morning.

After he finished his sandwich, Tom pulled out the book that he kept in his pack and whiled away the afternoon reading and basking in the bright sun. As usual, he kicked back, put his head on his pack and took a little nap. Deer hunting was the furthest thing from his mind. He hadn't even loaded his old Ruger rifle. With a start, around four o'clock he awoke from the strangest dream. With very little wasted effort, he slowly reached for his rifle, quietly opened the rolling block and slipped a cartridge in the magazine. Without really knowing why, he scanned the ridge line with his small binoculars and detected movement at the very top of the mountain. He switched to his scope on the rifle for better visibility and saw the biggest deer he ever seen beginning his decent. The animal was enormous, with a rack of horns that looked like an elk. It was heading down a brushy cut right toward Tom's little field. If that deer stays on track, he thought, I'm going to have him right in my lap!

With his 8-power scope, Tom watched the deer as he drifted in and out of the brush on the way to the broom straw field. It took forever, it seemed, before the monster mule deer emerged from the brushy cut that had acted like a highway leading to Tom. When the deer got to the edge of the field, he paused without any idea that a 30-06 rifle was zeroed in on his chest. He was so close that Tom could see the big brown eyes and steam coming from the deer's nostrils as he breathed in and out. Tom tightened his finger on the trigger and then for whatever reason changed his mind, stood up, said "bang" and watched the deer leap over the aspen blow-down and disappear.

He stood there for a long time, rifle at his side, then shouldered his pack and headed down the mountain for the last time.

When he reached the valley floor, he looked back toward his little pasture and saw an eagle, bright in the setting sun, soar over the ridge.

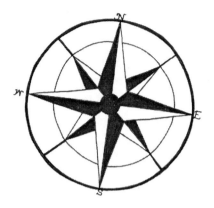

All Is Not Lost

Lost. Most of us have been lost at one time. It could be as simple as looking for a friend's home in a strange town, or trying to find a particular store in an unfamiliar shopping center, or driving on a road trip to another part of the country. It's not a regular occurrence in today's world of GPS, map quest, and smart phones, but it still happens; and most of the time, it's only an inconvenience made right by asking directions. Many males have a hard time asking how to get somewhere, but in the end and to save a lot of miles, I have pulled the car over to the side of the road and reluctantly asked whoever was handy how to get where I'm going.

Getting directions. Now there's another real grin. Have you ever noticed how people give directions? One helpful Samaritan offering advice is funny enough, but two at the same time can turn into a stand-up comedy routine. Three willing advisers might send you back to the car to find your destination by dead reckoning. A good example would be a road trip way back one summer when I was a college student. It started out innocently enough, and as most good trips, it was a spur of the moment thing.

Cliff Blue and I were lounging around, killing time at his father's lake cabin in Pinebluff. It was a typical Moore County summer day, soft breezes swaying the pines and cumulus clouds floating like so many cotton balls. We were kicked back, feet up on the railing of the screen porch, watching the lake right in front of the cabin. Fish made little breaks in the surface, feeding on the latest hatch of the day. "We should break out the fly rods and go down there and catch some of those fish. I mean they're aching to bite a good fly."

"It's too hot," Blue replied. He got up, went in the cabin and grabbed a beer from the cooler. "You want a beer?"

"Nah, I'm good."

He came back, sat down in a rocker, sighed and said, "Bryant, I'm bored."

"Well, what do you want me to do about it? I said we should go fishing."

"It's too blasted hot. We would melt out there."

He took a big slug of his beer and said, "I got it. We need a road trip. The weekend is coming. We can leave Friday afternoon when we get off work and go up to see Charlie Merrill. You know the railroad moved him to the mountains, I think to a little town called Saluda. It'll be a lot cooler on the Blue Ridge."

Charles Merrill, a former high school classmate, worked for the Southern Railroad Company and was based at Saluda Mountain right outside Asheville.

"That could be a good trip," I agreed. "Your car or mine?"

"Let's take mine. I don't feel like buying fifteen quarts of oil."

My old '40 Chevrolet had a penchant for using oil. I was scheduled to get the engine rebuilt later that summer. On this trip we were high in the mountains, as lost as the proverbial southern boy on his first adventure in New York City.

"Blue, you'd better stop and ask somebody where we are. We've been roaming around these mountains for hours. It'll be morning soon."

Blue slowed to a stop at an ancient coin laundry. Two old guys sitting in slat-back chairs were leaning against the building. We hesitantly approached them and Blue said, "Evening, folks. We're on the way to Saluda and seem to be lost, wonder if you can point us in the right direction?"

Both of them looked at us as if we were aliens from another planet. One leaned over, spat out a huge chaw of tobacco, stared at Blue, and said. "We knowed you was lost. You drove by here three times. Which way is your machine afacing?"

Blue looked at me with his mouth open then back at the old mountaineer and then at the car. He pointed at it and said, "It's facing that way, but it can turn around."

Dave Gardner in one of his comedy routines could have used the directions given by those two old guys.

We made it to Saluda just in time for the Coon Dog Festival, sort of a county fair with rides, good food, square dancing and all kinds of fun. We had a great time until some of the local good old boys accused us of "messing around with their women folk." We left town in a hurry, but that's another story.

I've only been really lost a time or two. I'm talking the gut wrenching, scared to death lost that can only occur in the middle of a vast wilderness. One experience was in the Wasatch Mountains of Utah. Four of us were on a mule deer hunt adventure for about eight or ten days. We were using a small cabin in a little valley next to a looming rugged range of peaks that seemed to go on forever. Our routine was to get up before dawn, split up, individually choose a section of the range to climb, and hunt while we explored.

For the first three or four days, I would walk south on the valley floor until the early gray daylight of the morning would give me enough light to help me climb toward the top of the rise. Each day I would try to go farther into the wild, building stamina as I progressed toward what I thought was the top of the ridge, which would hopefully allow me to look down into another valley. The sixth day dawned cloudy and cold with a touch of sleet and snow in the air. It was exciting and we were optimistic that one of us would surely be lucky and get a deer. I didn't understand I had a problem until late in the morning. After topping the sixth ridge and not finding a spot to set up and hunt, I decided to backtrack to a likely clearing I'd discovered on my early morning climb. Then I could hunker down for the rest of the day. But which way was the clearing? I had been using the sun as a compass while hunting. The morning sun was in my face when I climbed, and the afternoon sun was in my face on the way back down the mountains. On this day, however, because of the clouds and promising bad weather, there was no sun, and suddenly I realized that I was turned around and didn't know which direction would lead me back to the little valley and the cabin.

Fortunately, my Boy Scout training came in handy. The number one rule when lost in the wilderness is not to panic. I remembered the directions in the scout handbook and decided to sit, drink some water, have a little snack and see if I could recognize any landmarks. Easier said than done when snow is falling and possible help, in the form of a search party, wouldn't come until nightfall. Like an idiot, I'd forgot and left my compass at home, meaning to pick up another during the trip. That hadn't happened.

My bleached bones could still be weathering on top of a ridge of the Wasatch, but as luck would have it, along with many silent prayers and some not so silent, the sun peeked out from a dark cloud bank long enough to enable me to follow shadows all the way to the valley floor and the cabin. Older and wiser by the experience, I'm never in strange woods without a compass anymore. But I still have a hard time asking directions.

The Big Play

It never fails. Every time I watch a professional baseball game on television, I wonder when and where America's national sport left me behind. It was a rainy afternoon early in the spring season when I randomly flipped on the tube and caught the first couple of innings of the Texas Rangers playing somebody. It could have been a team from Florida since they had some kind of fish in their name. The game was boring, so I turned it off and decided to ride down to the farm I lease for hunting to see what was going to be planted this growing season.

I couldn't get the TV game out of my mind, though, so on the way south through Aberdeen I made a side trip and drove by what used to be the baseball field for Aberdeen High School. I did this several years ago when another bout of nostalgia got me thinking about the days I played ball in high school and college. The little field is still there, now morphed into a makeshift soccer stadium.

I'm the first to admit, as I enter the famed golden years (which actually means you'd better enjoy the time left, buddy, because there aren't that many more days left on your earthly calendar), professional players are not the same. They are bigger, faster, perhaps more talented, and they sure do make a whole lot more money than the ones of my era, but it just doesn't look as if they're having a lot of fun.

In my day, we had Mickey Mantle and Roger Maris and the great season when they competed with each other to break Babe Ruth's home run record. Other famous names tossed around the old horsehide: folks like Dizzy Dean, Whitey Ford, Roy Campanella, Ted Williams, Stan Musial, Willie Mays and later North Carolina's own Catfish Hunter. They were some of the best who played the game, and they looked as if they were having a good time, not just making a big paycheck.

Our Aberdeen High School Red Devils also had some heavyweight names on the senior squad, or at least we thought so: Jimmy Veasey, H.B. Ritter, Sonny Smith, and David Ruble. We didn't have a big team in numbers but more than made up for it in talent and, more importantly, fun.

Veasey, a fiery redhead and super athlete, played third base when he wasn't catching. He handled the hot corner with all the aplomb of a Brooks Robinson. Ritter and I went way back, having played on the same little league team. He could hit the ball a mile and played left field like a gazelle. Smith was a natural. He pitched and also spelled Veasey at catching. They were like peanut butter and jelly. Together they played havoc with the competition.

Ruble was the team leader and when he was in the field, we were all focused. He played center field, and his last-minute unbelievable catches and talent at bat won many a ball game for us.

Our coach, Bill Russell, a great individual, put up with a lot of shenanigans from his team and seemed to enjoy us as much as we did him.

The team was no slouch at the plate either. Several of us had a batting average of 400 or better. I believe H.B. Ritter ended the season as our number one hitter, batting almost 500. The competition at the plate was fierce, and we all tried to come away from each game with a little higher batting average. Every baseball player from the youngest little leaguer to the most seasoned World Series competitor dreams of what I like to call the Big Play. It could be an impossible task, in the field or at bat, that somehow wins the game for the team. It actually happened to me a couple of times.

In my senior year we were playing Vass Lakeview High School, a school smaller than Aberdeen, if that was possible. We were visitors at their little stadium beside the school. The field was nothing more than a dirt patch outlined with lime to indicate the boundaries. There was a partial fence that marked center field and part of right field, but left field was open and stretched all the way to the tree line. It was as if they had started the fence and had yet to complete it.

Nothing seemed to go right for us. We left men on base and made a couple of errors that enabled them to score two runs. When we came to bat in the bottom of the ninth, we had one last chance to tie or win. First, Ritter hit a long drive to right field that the outfielder caught right at the fence. Next up, Ruble hit a line drive and slid into second with a double. Smith popped up to the second baseman for out number two. Veasey was walked to put two on base, Lewis hit a grounder that the short stop bobbled, and we had the bases loaded with two outs and yours truly coming to bat.

The first pitch was high and outside for a ball. The second, I hit foul down the left field line. I took another ball low and inside. I was ahead of the count and the second base coach signaled that I should take a pitch, which I did for a strike. The count was two balls and two strikes. The next pitch was high and inside for ball number three. One more pitch and the game could be over, or I could be a hero. Full count, the bases loaded, two outs and the pitcher fires a screamer right down the center of the plate, and I unload on it. The ball sails right down the left field line where there is no fence, and the left fielder at the last possible second dives and makes a miraculous catch to end the game. As I rounded second on the way to what I thought would be a homer, all I could do was cuss the lack of a fence in left field. I missed my chance for the big play. The team commiserated the missing fence and our lack of luck on that pretty spring day, but we had fun. Later that season we went on to play Southern Pines for the championship, which we ironically lost, two to zip. That was my last game for old AHS. I had the opportunity to play in college and had another chance for the big play, but that's another story for another time.

Three Mornings in the Spring Woods

TURKEY HUNT - Day One

We shut down our vehicles in the little cut in the stand of pines, got out and softly pushed the doors closed. It was that time in the morning between night and day. There was just enough grayness for us to see to get ready, but dawn was still an hour away.

"Hey Tom, you want an egg sandwich? I made 'em this morning, still warm."

"Sure, and I brought some coffee. You want some?"

"Brought my own. Thanks though."

The sky was rapidly getting light in the east.

"We ought to be hearing something pretty soon," Rich said as we munched down on our sandwiches. The words were just out his mouth when a turkey gobbled and we both turned our heads toward the sound like bird dogs on point. Rich looked at me and we both grinned. He said, "I just lost my appetite. Let's load up and get on over there."

The over there he was talking about was at least a quarter of a mile from where we had parked our trucks. The gobble sounded again as we grabbed our gear and headed that way.

"That rascal is still on the roost," Rich said as we moved quickly but quietly toward the sound. "We'll ease down that gas line road and set up back in the trees."

We made the hike to the tree line in record time, picked our spots under a couple of big pines, put on our camouflaged head nets and gloves, and loaded the shotguns.

The turkey gobbled again. Rich was behind me a few yards using his mouth call.

"If the turkey comes this way," he whispered, "I want you to be the first to miss." He chuckled softly and adjusted his dove stool.

Rich clucked a few times with his call and the old gobbler hollered like he had just discovered the turkey playboy mansion. He's coming this way, I thought as my heart elevated to my throat.

About that time, I heard a loud call down toward the creek. What the heck? I heard it again. It sounded as if someone was trying to call like an owl, or maybe more like a drunk blue heron. He called again. Every time whoever it was made that awful racket, the turkey would gobble. The fake owl got closer, making more noise as he came. When he got to about fifty yards behind us, the fellow pulled out his box call and started yelping.

Rich and I remained silent, hoping the turkey would come anyway. It didn't work. The next time I heard the gobbler, he was hightailing it over the ridge, probably heading to the next county. Rich and I sat silently until the interloper moved back toward the creek.

"That happens sometimes," Rich said as he quietly edged up behind me. We might as well go back and finish our sandwiches. It's probably over for today."

"Whoever he was, he messed up a sure thing." I said.

"Nah," he replied. "There is no such thing as a sure thing in the turkey hunting business. It was fun to hear him gobble like that, though. Maybe we'll get him next time."

TURKEY HUNT - Day Two

"Tom, let's go back to the same spot where we were the other day and set up around that deer food patch. I think the gobblers have hens with them and won't move until later."

The day before, a warm front had come through and the humidity was kicking in with heat right on its heels. I was already sweating as we trudged down the road. Rich hunkered down on the west side of the freshly planted food patch and I went over to the east side, back in the tree line a bit, and put on all my camouflage stuff. Rich clucked a few times and then we were quiet and listened as the area awoke from its spring snooze.

Unfortunately, we weren't the only ones enjoying this warm weather. Mosquitoes began to attack in force. There is nothing more irritating than mosquitoes buzzing around your ears. Even though I had on a head net and a hat, my concentration went out the window. I slowly raised my hand to slap at a mosquito and looked toward the south end of the cutover.

There stood probably the biggest turkey I'd ever seen. He saw me at the same time and disappeared as quickly as he had appeared. In a few minutes, Rich came across the little plowed area and said with a sheepish grin on his face. "Did you see him?"

"Yep, and he saw me. Let's get out of these mosquitoes and talk about it."

Rich could tell I was disappointed that I had made the ultimate faux pas, moving when a turkey is near. A turkey might be a dumb bird, but he can see an eye blink at fifty yards.

"Don't worry about it, Bubba. We'll get him next time."

TURKEY HUNT - Day Three

Rich, my friend and turkey-hunting guide, is an amazing athlete and sportsman. He was a four-letter man in high school sports: football, baseball, basketball and track. He did the same thing in college, earning a scholarship playing football, baseball and basketball. He's no slouch on the golf course either, shooting his age more often than not. In the woods he's probably as good as I've seen, and I've seen a bunch. The afternoon after we saw the big turkey (the one that got away), we decided to do a little more reconnoitering for the hunt we'd planned for the following morning. After checking out the woods for likely set-up points, we headed back to the vehicles.

I asked Rich about his last birthday as we hiked up the sand hill to our starting point. "Rich, you're eighty years old and get along better in the woods than someone half your age. How do you do it?"

"I don't do numbers, Tom. So many people reach a certain age and they figure they need to hit the rocking chair. I get up in the morning and if I want to do something, I do it."

And "do it" is right. A typical day for Rich, such as the day before, went like this: up at 4:30 AM, turkey hunt until 8:30, go to the golf course and play 18 holes, have lunch, and go to the dog kennels to work his champion English Pointers. Then home for supper and get ready to do it again the next day. Does the fellow ever get tired?

Our turkey hunt today was unsuccessful, but we still have three more days left in turkey season, but I really don't care if we get one or not. I've had a wonderful time this spring watching nature come alive after a hard winter. Where else could you see what Rich and I witnessed this morning as we were loading up after a hunt?

We were standing near the vehicles making plans for the next day when a ruby-throated hummingbird flew right between us, hovered a moment, then zipped out of sight.

"Man," Rich said as he looked at me in amazement. "That made the day."

It not only made my day, it was the peak of a wonderful few mornings in the woods.

Dove Season

I pulled the old Bronco into the pines and circled around to park close to the ancient dead longleaf. I had noticed the year before that doves loved to rest on the branches before dropping into the field to feed. This is one of my favorite times of year, one week before dove season and the beginning of bird hunting. It never changes. In all the years I've been in the woods and before each dove season, I still feel like a kid on Christmas Eve.

I eased out of the truck and set my dove stool back in the pines a bit, primarily for shade but also not to disturb hungry doves. The weather had been sizzling, always is, I thought. September can be as hot as August. Weather-wise they sort of run together, but at sundown a slight difference can be discerned when the white hot sun slowly approaches the horizon. It's something to do with the shadows and colors and smells and sounds as the scorched earth starts to rest, beginning a slow move to fall and another season.

About ten or fifteen doves flew tree high over the cut corn field and angled toward the dead pine as if on strings. I stayed motionless and watched as they were joined by several more. They effortlessly glided from the tree to the field and began picking and grazing like barnyard chickens. I sat quietly and watched as the birds on the ground were joined by more of their confederate gray cousins. In just a few minutes, it was amazing to see the field carpeted with birds, little heads darting back and forth with metronome regularity.

As quickly as they came and as if a uniform signal had been given, they all rose as one and headed to the trees surrounding the pond, probably to roost for the evening. I continued to sit in the same spot to see what would happen at dusk when evening would settle on the farm. An owl called near the beaver pond and purple martins began darting across the sky catching bugs for supper.

Thinking of food, I meandered back to the Bronco, opened the back, and grabbed a pack of nabs from my gunning bag and a cold libation from the cooler. I wondered how many times I had done this. It's been a bunch. September and dove season go together like December and Christmas. As the years have rolled by, I've found that narrowing a happening down to a month has become too much of a burden, so I've decided to just use seasons as a calendar. Here we are rapidly pushing August behind us and roaring on into September and fall, and yet we still have about a month left of summer.

So let's start with summer. I'll think of a great memory from a summer past, then one from a fall, likewise a memorable happening from winter and spring. Forget the months, the seasons will take care of themselves. Let's give it a try.

SUMMER, that's easy. It was the mid '60s, I was fresh out of the Marine Corps and back in school, rambling, trying like crazy to grab some direction from somewhere, when I met this cute co-ed. She was a student at the University of North Carolina at Greensboro (formerly Woman's College of the University of North Carolina), majoring in elementary education. Eight months later, we were married and have lived a wonderful life. This August we will have been together for over fifty years. I still remember what my dad said the first time he met Linda. "Son, the best day's work you've ever done is to convince this lovely girl to be your bride. You're a lucky man."

I heard the owl again. It had moved from the beaver pond into the pines behind me and was probably getting ready for its evening hunt. The sun was about gone and shadows from the trees across the cut field loomed my way. I could see a couple of deer ease out into the edge and slowly begin to graze. Tonight there would be a full moon, and I decided to sit for a spell and see what would happen when it came up over the eastern tree line.

As the grayness of sundown gave way to the dark of night, the moon slowly added its brightness to the scene. More deer came out into the open and I could see white tails flash sporadically. There were probably ten or fifteen small does and some young ones in the mix. A couple of the youngest would scamper about playing deer tag, their moms grazing contentedly. There is one thing I've learned in my years of living, and probably the reason I'm a Presbyterian: good and bad things happen sometimes, with no rhyme or reason. They were just meant to be, and that's something I think about in the fall.

My dad, one of the finest men I've ever known, died in the fall, October to be exact. He was fifty-five years old. A job related illness, lung cancer, grabbed him just as he was ready to launch a more fun time for himself and my mom. A part of Tom Brokow's greatest generation, my father served in the navy during World War II and, like many others of that time, came home after saving the world and got down to the business of providing a living for his family.

Every now and then when I pass a mirror or catch a reflection of myself in a store window, I see my dad. It's a funny sensation. As my mom often tells me, you have to take the bad with the good; and in keeping with that old saying, our son Tommy was born a year later. My dad died in October, Tommy was born the following year in November. Both fall happenings, one terribly bad and one unbelievably good. Tom never met his granddad, but it's uncanny how much alike they are.

The moon was now fully over the horizon and I decided to fire up the old Bronco and head home. I realized placing memories in seasons worked pretty well. Or better yet, I thought, and a whole lot less complicated, let the memories come when they will, who cares about the time line. The important thing is creating them; each season has room for many more.

On Beaver Pond

"Today my friends, we each have one day less, every one of us. And joy is the only thing that slows the clock." John D. MacDonald, *The Scarlet Ruse*

It was my favorite time of year. I don't know why I say that. Every season is my favorite, except that maybe fall has more in the plus column because of bird hunting, surf-fishing, and just the beauty of the great outdoors. In the fall, Mother Nature pulls out her most colorful palette and paints the landscape in brilliant hues of red, yellow, russet, and pine green, preparing nature for its long winter sleep and another beauty that's entirely different.

Earlier this past summer, during one of my many forays afield, I discovered, just by chance, a beaver pond way back off the beaten path, down close to a small creek where I hoped to do a little cane pole fishing. I was really far back in swamp country and being extra careful not to disturb "Mr. No Shoulders," an old native American term for snake, I was treading lightly. It had been fairly dry for a couple of weeks and farm crops and wildlife badly needed some rain, so the ground that would have been very marshy was passable. I hardly got my feet wet. But after stepping around over-grown areas and toting some unwieldy fishing poles, I decided to head back to the truck, drive over to the farm pond, and fish there.

As I angled back on the return path, I noticed to the west a general sloping where the land and vegetation seemed to be more vibrant. Walking slowly and being extra quiet not to alert wildlife, I discovered the beaver pond. It was a picture right out of Sporting Classics magazine. Alders were thick on the banks and hickory trees and oaks and even some cypress completed the picture of a perfect undisturbed wild habitat created by one of my favorite animals, the industrious beaver. It was late in the afternoon so I abandoned the idea of fishing and decided to sit and watch a bit to see what game was using the pond. I had just settled down with my back against a big longleaf pine when two wood ducks, a hen and a drake, darted through the alders and skidded across the water right in front of me. They swam for a couple of minutes and then leaped straight up, kicked in the afterburner, and jetted out the far end of the pond. They must have seen me, I thought as they climbed out of sight.

As soon as the ducks were gone, a pair of deer, a doe and a new fawn, materialized on the far side and nosed down to the water to drink. They stood for a minute or two and disappeared back into the forest as if they had never been there.

Three beaver swam close to where the deer had been. They were dragging freshly cut alders through the water, probably to reinforce their dam. My new discovery was so unbelievably pristine, it was hard for me to leave; but sunset was on the way, and I needed good light for my trek back to the truck. I made mental notes of the location of the beaver pond, resolving to come back as soon as I could; but as in a lot of my endeavors lately, I was delayed.

It was October before I could visit the pond again. A northwestern front had moved through the area the evening before, leaving behind the first real cool snap of the season. I was on my way to revisit the pond and was really up for a big day in the woods. The deep blue sky was the perfect backdrop for the russet colored dogwoods accented with yellow hickory leaves. I pulled the truck into the woods a little way and grabbed my gunning bag and shotgun from the back. The shotgun was one of my favorites, a 28-gauge Remington 870 that I had rigged with a sling so I could carry it over my shoulder.

Linda, my bride, had given me the little gun for my birthday many years ago and it became the one I used the most when I was going to be in the field for an extended time. Birthdays. They were rolling around pretty fast, it seemed. I had just celebrated one that really got my attention. It wasn't one with zeros, although those tend to amplify the speed of time. This one quartered the century and was a special event in my rush through life. It increased awareness of my own mortality. I recognized the route to the beaver pond right off the bat and moved off in that direction at a brisk pace.

I had plenty of time and had to keep telling myself that there was no train to catch and to slow down and enjoy the day. That was it, enjoy, and I thought of John MacDonald's quote in his book that I had just read, reread actually. "Joy is the only thing that slows the clock" in our rush to the end, or as a lot of us hope, the beginning.

I caught glimpses of water reflected by the overhead sun and slowed my walk to a crawl, so as not to disturb any animals that were enjoying the pond. Ironically, I came to the water at the same location I had on my first visit, propped my shotgun against the pine and sat down using the tree for a backrest. The rest of the afternoon was a blur. It was as if the area wildlife planned to put on a show for me and used the little pond as a stage. I saw beaver, deer, ducks, doves, a pair of otters, and even a bobcat made a special appearance. They didn't notice me, or if they did, they didn't care. They went about their business as if I was part of the scenery and belonged, just as they did.

It was an exceptional time in the backcountry, and all too soon my special day was gone. I had a real knowledge of the pond now, having walked the northern perimeter from the dam to the creek. It was about five acres and was situated in the swamp bottom. The beaver used the lay of the land to build one of the best nature habitats I've ever seen. I came out of the woods near the truck just as a full moon was coming up over the eastern pines. I got a drink out of the cooler in the back, grabbed a sack of peanuts out of my gunning bag, leaned up against the front fender and watched as a pair of Canada geese, silhouetted against the moon, flew honking toward to the pond, probably to roost.

What an experience. If MacDonald is right, and you can slow down the clock that's moving toward our inevitable demise by enjoying life, I dang near stopped the thing today.

Ducks Revisited

It's easy to see how I was led down the road to my addiction. It began slowly, not something that would grab me overnight, but in the beginning I was sucked in just as surely and steadily as a beagle on the trail of a rabbit. You see, I can say it now, and all the experts will tell you that the hardest part of admitting to an addiction is recognizing it and taking ownership. So for the record, I'm a recovering duck hunter. It all began in the little town of Pinebluff. I was twelve or thirteen years old with a bicycle, a curly-coated retriever dog named Smut and a 12-gauge J.C. Higgins shotgun, a Christmas gift from my dad. During hunting season, Smut and I would spend a lot of time in the woods. Usually the scenario would work like this: Dad would take my shotgun and Smut to work with him at the ice plant right outside of Aberdeen. I was in the sixth grade at Aberdeen Elementary, and after school I would hike down to the plant, do my homework, whistle up Smut, grab my shotgun and walk the railroad tracks back to Pinebluff hunting all the way.

In those days I was a hunter, period. I wasn't partial to any species. If it was in season, it was game. A typical afternoon bag might include a couple of squirrels, a dove or two, maybe a quail, or even and not unusual, a rabbit. When I got home, a little after sundown, I'd clean the game and Mom would put it in the freezer for us to enjoy later. Then on a special weekend and depending on the diversity of what I had harvested, Mom would prepare a wild game feast fit for a king, or better yet a young boy who was extremely proud of his success in the field. I hunted for two or three years before I ever bagged my first duck. It was a perfect day that still resonates in my mind. A couple of weeks before Christmas with a cold gray sky promising snow, Smut and I were on the game trail again. Feeling a little adventurous, I decided to hunt the tracks south of Pinebluff toward Addor. Smut and I rarely hunted this area, usually concentrating our efforts on the land north of our little village.

It was a silent morning. Most of the wildlife was hunkered down preparing for the bad weather promised later in the day. Every now and then, a little sleet would spit from the lowering sky, nature's warning of what was to come. We ambled on down the tracks taking little side diversions to see what game we might be able to jump. It was slow, not much going on. Even Smut who was always running far ahead stayed close as if anticipating the weather.

About a half-mile from the tracks, I noticed what looked to be a swampy area and thinking that perhaps squirrels would be active around water, especially if it wasn't frozen, I led Smut through heavy brush toward what turned out to be a little beaver pond. I could see open water reflecting out of the shadows of big cypress trees, and I decided to just watch for a minute and see if anything was roaming in the tall branches. Ripples on the water alerted me to a movement on the far side of the pond, and I crouched down and grabbed Smut to keep him close. I had just got to my knees when two wood ducks exploded from the far side and flew right at me. I don't remember how I did it, but I fired two shots from the 12-gauge, and down crashed two wood ducks. The silence after the blast of the shotgun was deafening, and Smut and I stood for a second or two in awe. Then the celebration started.

You would have thought that I had just brought down two Canada geese. I dashed to the spot where I thought one duck had fallen, and

Smut raced to the other side of the pond for the second one. I found the drake as Smut came crashing back through the brush with the hen. He looked up at me with the little duck in his jaws as if to say, "Hey boss, this is pretty good stuff. Why haven't we done this before?"

It was a magical moment, two ducks in the bag, Christmas holidays right around the corner, and it began to snow. I think we floated home rather than walked, we were so proud. Mother bragged on us sufficiently, promising to cook a duck dinner later during the holidays, and Dad expressed his wonder that a boy and his dog accomplished what many adults had trouble doing.

That was the beginning of my duck hunting adventures. As I said, the addiction was insidious. I stopped hunting other game and concentrated on ducks. Smut and I would head to the swamp or any place that might harbor ducks and would sit and watch and wait. I didn't get another duck that year. In the off-season, we would scout likely waters, and I read everything I could about waterfowling. My gear in those days consisted of military surplus camouflaged clothing, a pair of leaky hip boots that I acquired from an uncle who had feet about the size of mine, and marsh-brown feed sacks that I tied together to make a portable blind.

We trained. I did everything I could to transform Smut into a duck-retrieving machine. It didn't work. I would throw a stick that I tried to rig like a duck to get him to bring it back to me. He would race to it and look back as if to say, "This is nothing but a stick. What do you want me to do with it?" It was funny. Smut wasn't a training, make-work, kind of retriever but in the woods when we were hunting, he was all business and we spent many happy times afield.

Those early days ushered in the future, and I became a dedicated waterfowling hunter acquiring more gear, the latest in waders and clothing, boats, decoys, and gun dogs. If it had to do with duck hunting, I wanted it. And then a couple of years ago after spending an inordinate amount of time and money traveling to our impoundments at Lake Mattamuskeet and having little luck in bringing home the bacon, as it were,

I hung up my waders. I mothballed my duck boat fleet. I stored all my decoys on shelves in the garage. I put the steel shotgun shells in the far corner of my gun cabinet and considered selling my special Remington 870 12-gauge. For the first time in over fifty years, I didn't buy a required duck stamp to attach to my regular hunting license making me legal to hunt ducks. The addiction was gone, cold turkey.

But the other day while I was out at the little farm I lease to dove hunt, I watched as two wood ducks, a hen and a drake, rocketed into the pond that's on the far side of the field. On the way home, I stopped at Walmart and bought a duck stamp.

Whistling Wings

I was up in the roost, a little apartment above our garage where I go to write and hang out when I need to get out of the way of the vacuum cleaner and my bride, Linda.

I was sorting through duck hunting gear from my last trip to Lake Mattamuskeet. Shotguns, waders, heavy waterproof hunting coats, shotgun shells, duck calls, hunting trousers—you name it and if it pertains to duck hunting, it was in a pile in the roost.

Duck season ushered in a new kind of hunting for me in 2016 and January of the New Year. In the past, I was used to running my own show, so to speak. A group of us, six to be exact, leased impoundments right on the Pamlico Sound. Also included in the lease was a small house that served as our lodge. For a few years, the arrangement worked okay but then a series of bad weather events flooded the impoundments with salt water, making them useless for growing corn, and the ducks went elsewhere. At the same time, our little lodge was invaded with a legion of mice, making the place uninhabitable, so we gave up our efforts and I didn't duck hunt in that area for a while.

I missed the wilds of Hyde County, though, so last summer when my good friend Art called after a visit to Engelhard, scouting for a new duck hunting venue, I was excited. "Hey, Tom, How you doing, sport?"

"Great, Art! Good to hear from you. What are you up to?"

"Jack, John and I have been scouting around Hyde County, looking for a spot for us to hang our duck-hunting hats, and we think we've found it. You interested?"

Needless to say I was, and they added me to the group. The hunt would be handled sort of the way I was introduced to the area. We would use a guide and his impoundments located right on the northern end of the lake. The guide would take care of all the details, which I wasn't used to; but hey, I thought, I'm not getting any younger and maybe an easy hunt like this would be nice.

The weeks rolled by and all of a sudden, it was time to round up all my duck-hunting stuff, load up the Cruiser and head east. The ride to Hyde County from Southern Pines was a trip of extremes, up through Raleigh and all the break-neck traffic trying to get nowhere fast, and then with a sigh of relief, I eased across the Pungo River onto the "Road Less Traveled," which is the motto of Hyde County. When I crossed the river, I pulled into a little gravel parking area right on the other side of the bridge and walked back to see if anything had changed since my last visit. An osprey was fishing, diving into the water with a splash, and with a fish in his claws, headed back across the tree line bordering the river to eat lunch.

Then I heard them before I could see them. High above were hundreds of snow geese, just little spots against the washed-out blue of the winter sky, their soft plaintive calls an indication of the altitude at which they were flying.

Excited, I fired up the Cruiser and motored toward Engelhard and the pair of cabins that would serve as our headquarters for the next four days. Art, John, Jack, and Art's son, Michael, were an hour or more behind me, so I got to the cabins first, unloaded some gear and waited for their arrival and the beginning of good times.

I had just sat down in a swing on the porch overlooking the Pamlico

Sound when the troops pulled in the drive. In no time, all their gear was unloaded, and John, the gourmet chef of the group, had staked out which cabin and kitchen he would use for his culinary efforts. I have been hunting with John for years and have been fortunate to experience many meals prepared by this excellent cook. We all looked forward to his expertise in the kitchen, always a high point of the hunt.

After completing the details of unloading and who was to use which cabin, Art called the guide to get our marching orders for the next day and also see if we could check out the evening flight into the impoundments. The guide said he would meet us at his barn and take us to the dike to watch, so we took care of some last minute details and everyone loaded into Michael's big Suburban for the fifteen-minute ride to our morning rendezvous, hopefully, with ducks.

The gray evening was heavily overcast with low clouds spitting rain, and although we couldn't see the ducks, we sure could hear them. Our guide told us, "If the weather holds, we should wear 'em out at sunrise."

We drove back to the cabins full of anticipation.

Five AM came early after an evening of good fellowship and John's great cooking, but it didn't take long to trudge to the Suburban, heavily loaded with guns and gear. On the way to the impoundments, Michael was commiserating about his lack of experience duck hunting. This was his first time in a blind. Michael has a very responsible position with Wells Fargo Bank and spends a lot of time on the job. The rest of the guys told him that duck hunting was a snap and he should be really good at it. Jokingly, they said, "Just watch Bryant and try to do the opposite."

We met the guide and trooped to the blind in good order. The weather was still blowing out of the northeast with a heavy mist. We hunkered down under cover and waited for legal shooting time. Whistling wings could be heard overhead as ducks started coming off the roost heading to the lake. You could almost taste the excitement. The guide whispered, "Okay, it's time, get ready."

A pair of widgeons swung by out front and one fell to our guns. Another pair, wood ducks this time, came from the right and flew straight out. Michael's gun roared and both ducks fell. Two ducks, one shot. Even the guide celebrated and gave Michael a high five. "See," I said and laughed.

"This duck hunting isn't that hard."

The morning went by in a blur as ducks came to the blind; but to me, the most incredible sight was the tundra swans coming off the lake, literally by the thousands. They were flying treetop high over the blind, and the sounds they made calling in those impossible numbers I'll probably never hear again in my lifetime. It was one of nature's most incredible sights, and I surely won't forget it.

I looked out the window of the roost and watched as a pair of cardinals flew to the bird feeder. Well, I thought, here it is February, and there's duck hunting stuff everywhere. Time to put it all away until next season and see if I can put together some fishing gear. We're leaving for Florida and Chokoloskee Island soon and the folks down there say the fishing is great.

Acknowledgments

So how did my book get to be a book? I'm very thankful for all the people who have helped along the way. Naming everyone seems impossible, but I'm going to give it a shot, at least hit the tip of the iceberg.

First and foremost, my family really got me started. I was lucky to be born in the south where families and traditions go hand in hand. My dad and mom taught me the important things in life including love for family, God and country. My parents and grandparents let me learn by doing, and I had many adventures and experiences during my young years. My grandfather took me under his wing when I was just a youngster and showed me the importance of the great outdoors, how to have fun in it and how it deserved my respect. I spent many delightful hours learning about nature from his perspective while paddling a river skiff or following along behind him and a birddog. My brother and sisters were always supportive, and we grew up loving the same things about the outdoors.

Linda, my bride, as she became known through my columns, encouraged me to write, and she became my chief editor. She read what I wrote and helped me with ideas when the muse refused to visit. After I talked her into it, she also agreed to illustrate the columns and paint a watercolor for the cover.

My son, Tommy, followed me across numerous dove fields and backwoods. When we weren't bird hunting, we were fishing. He became a great outdoorsman in his own right, maybe even better than his old dad.

Good friends and hunting buddies are too numerous to mention in their entirety, but I will talk about the ones I call my roving editors. They read the columns and picked the ones they liked best. Tom Bobo, Bryan Pennington, Art Rogers, Jack Spencer, John Vernon, and Rich Warters have heard a lot of these tales on hunting trips, some of them more than once. One of their favorite quips to me is "Bryant, you've got to get new stories or new friends."

I got in the newspaper business during the latter days of linotype and letterpresses, and I was fortunate to learn and grow under some of the finest leaders in the industry. From the very beginning, my chief ambition was to have my own newspaper, and that happened in 1977. A friend, Jim Lasley, and I began a small weekly, *The City-County Newspaper*.

I was fortunate to get to know Frank Daniels, Jr., one of the last great icons in the industry and the publisher and owner of *The News and Observer* in Raleigh. Ironically, later in my career, I worked for Frank at his Southern Pines newspaper, *The Pilot*. His nephew, my friend, David Woronoff, became publisher. I was able to help him as advertising director and, at the same time, begin writing an outdoor column for the paper.

David is an amazingly talented gentleman. During his tenure as publisher, he created three major magazines, *Pinestraw* in Moore County, *O.Henry* in Guilford County, and *Salt* in Wilmington. Later he and his partners acquired Business North Carolina Magazine, a statewide publication.

Jim Dodson, the editor of these magazines and a New York Times best-selling author, became a good friend and urged me become PineStraw's sporting life columnist. Andie Rose, the creative director of the magazines, lent her talents, which by the way are second to none, by providing art and her design expertise.

Hunter Chase, the sports editor of *The Pilot*, accepted the many columns I submitted and encouraged me to write more. For that, I'm indebted to him.

Last but not least is a young lady I got to know when she came to *The Pilot* a few years ago as an intern. Kimberly Daniels Taws now manages The Country Bookshop and has accepted the dubious duty of serving as my literary agent. If I could bottle and sell her energy and enthusiastic attitude, I would be a wealthy man. She has looked after the book from its conception to the printed copy, and I owe her tremendous thanks.

The name of this book, *Southern Sunrises*, comes from my many mornings watching nature in all its glory. I've seen more sunrises in the field than I can count, from frosty steel grey in the winter to blistering white-hot in the summer. Every one of them has been different.

I hope you enjoy the following pages. Perhaps I'll run across you in the woods early one morning when we can watch a southern sunrise together and share some good stories.

CPSIA information can be obtained
at www.ICGtesting.com
Printed in the USA
LVOW12s1000081017
551660LV00003B/482/P